PENGUIN CLASSICS

THE LAIS OF MARIE DE FRANCE

GLYN S. BURGESS studied French at St John's College, Oxford. He then took his MA at McMaster University, Hamilton, Ontario, and went on to do a doctorate at the Sorbonne. He has taught at Queen's University, Ontario, at the University of South Carolina, and from 1971 at the University of Liverpool. He has now retired and is Professor Emeritus. His interests lie in early medieval French literature, especially in the relationship between literature and society. In addition to the present volume, he has translated *The Song of Roland* for Penguin Classics, and he has published widely on twelfth-century courtly literature, especially on the *Lais* of Marie de France. His publications include *Contribution à l'étude du vocabulaire pré-courtois* (1977), *Marie de France: an Analytical Bibliography* (1977; first supplement 1986, second supplement 1997), *Chrétien de Troyes; Erec et Enide* (1984), *The Lais of Marie de France: Text and Context* (1987), *The Old French Narrative Lay: an Analytical Bibliography* (1995) and *Two Medieval Outlaws: Eustace the Monk and Fouke Fitz Waryn* (1997). He has been associated since its inception in the mid 1970s with the International Courtly Literature Society, of which he was President from 1989 to 1995.

KEITH BUSBY is Professor of French at the University of Wisconsin, Madison. He was previously Professor of Old French and Comparative Literature at the Universities of Leiden and Utrecht in the Netherlands. He was educated at Magdalen College, Oxford, and at the universities of York and Poitiers. His most recent publications include a critical edition of Chrétien de Troyes' *Perceval* and a critical guide to the same text (both in 1993). He also co-authored and edited the two-volume *The Manuscripts of Chrétien de Troyes* (1993). His current major interest is the study of medieval literature in its manuscript context.

The Lais of
Marie de France

TRANSLATED
WITH AN INTRODUCTION BY
Glyn S. Burgess and Keith Busby

Second Edition with two further lais
in the original Old French

PENGUIN BOOKS

PENGUIN BOOKS

Published by the Penguin Group
Penguin Books Ltd, 80 Strand, London WC2R ORL, England
Penguin Putnam Inc., 375 Hudson Street, New York, New York 10014, USA
Penguin Books Australia Ltd, 250 Camberwell Road, Camberwell, Victoria 3124, Australia
Penguin Books Canada Ltd, 10 Alcorn Avenue, Toronto, Ontario, Canada M4V 3B2
Penguin Books India (P) Ltd, 11 Community Centre, Panchsheel Park, New Delhi – 110 017, India
Penguin Books (NZ) Ltd, Cnr Rosedale and Airborne Roads, Albany, Auckland, New Zealand
Penguin Books (South Africa) (Pty) Ltd, 24 Sturdee Avenue, Rosebank 2196, South Africa

Penguin Books Ltd, Registered Offices: 80 Strand, London WC2R ORL, England

www.penguin.com

This translation first published 1986
Second edition published with updated Bibliography
and two further *lais Lanval* and *Chevrefoil* in the original Old French, 1999
Reprinted 2003
16

Translation and Introduction copyright © Glynn S. Burgess and Keith Busby, 1986, 1999
All rights reserved

Filmset in 10/12pt Monophoto Baskerville
Printed in England by Clays Ltd, St Ives plc

ISBN-13: 978-0-14-044759-0

CONTENTS

PREFACE TO THE SECOND EDITION ... 5

INTRODUCTION ... 7

TRANSLATORS' NOTE ... 37

PROLOGUE ... 41

I GUIGEMAR ... 43

II EQUITAN ... 56

III LE FRESNE ... 61

IV BISCLAVRET ... 68

V LANVAL ... 73

VI LES DEUX AMANZ ... 82

VII YONEC ... 86

VIII LAÜSTIC ... 94

IX MILUN ... 97

X CHAITIVEL ... 105

XI CHEVREFOIL ... 109

XII ELIDUC ... 111

NOTES ... 127

BIBLIOGRAPHY ... 129

INDEX OF PROPER NAMES ... 135

TEXT OF LANVAL ... 139

TEXT OF LAÜSTIC ... 156

TEXT OF CHEVREFOIL ... 161

PREFACE TO THE SECOND EDITION

A huge amount of material has been published on Marie de France since the appearance of the first edition of this translation. This new edition includes both an updated and expanded Bibliography and two new lays in the Old French original, *Lanval* and *Chevrefoil* (edited here by G. S. Burgess). *Lanval* is Marie's only truly Arthurian lay and it has English analogues in the form of *Sir Launfal* and *Sir Landevale*. *Chevrefoil* recounts an episode in the lives of Tristan and Iseut. The shortest of Marie's lays, it possesses considerable poetic intensity and gives rise to problems of interpretation which have exercised the minds of many readers over the years.

INTRODUCTION

An introduction of this sort usually starts with certain basic facts. When and where the author was born. What the principal biographical details are which might be relevant to his or her literary output. What exactly the author wrote and under what circumstances. What the relationship is between the material being presented and that of earlier authors or of writers contemporary with the author, on whom or by whom influence could have been exerted, in respect of genre, theme or textual details. Sadly, in the case of Marie de France none of this information can be given with certainty. We can assert with conviction that at least one poet by the name of Marie was writing in the second half of the twelfth century, but it is equally certain that the author who composed the lays contained in this volume was not called Marie de France. This appellation is first attested in the *Recueil de l'origine de la langue et poesie françoise* by Claude Fauchet (Paris, 1581, Book II, item 84). It has been used ever since as a convenient and attractive name for our author.

One must begin by examining the textual evidence. The tales which are translated in the present volume are found in a thirteenth-century manuscript in the British Library (Harley 978). These twelve short poems in Old French are included among a number of other items principally in Latin (there is, however, in the manuscript, a collection of fables in Old French). The twelve poems, which are preceded by a fifty-six-line Prologue, are in order: *Guigemar, Equitan, Le Fresne, Bisclavret, Lanval, Deus Amanz, Yonec, Laüstic, Milun, Chaitivel, Chevrefoil* and *Eliduc*. The text of the Harley manuscript (MS H) and the order in which the poems appear form the basis of most editions and several translations, including that found in the present volume. The poems were certainly not composed in this order, and some translators (for example E. Mason and H. F. Williams) prefer to select their own order. The tales are also found in four other manuscripts, only one of which (MS S, Paris, Bibliothèque Nationale, nouv. acq. fr. 1104) can be regarded as offering a substantial collection. Here the order is different and not all the poems are complete: *Guigemar, Lanval, Yonec, Chevrefoil, Deus Amanz* (vv. 1–159), *Bisclavret* (from v. 233), *Milun, Le Fresne, Equitan*. Another Paris manuscript (MS P, Bibliothèque Nationale, fr. 2168) contains *Yonec* (from v. 396), *Guigemar* and *Lanval*. Two further manuscripts, MS C (British Library, Cott. Vesp. B XIV) and MS Q (Bibliothèque Nationale, fr. 24432), contain *Lanval* and *Yonec* respectively. Thus only *Guigemar, Lanval* and *Yonec* occur in more than two manuscripts and *Laüstic, Chaitivel* and *Eliduc* are found just once. The Prologue, which prefaces the Harley collection, is absent from the other French manuscripts.

These short stories, varying in length from 118 lines (*Chevrefoil*) to 1,184 lines (*Eliduc*), with an average length of 477 lines, are traditionally called lays. The Prologue speaks of *lais* which the author had heard recited: *'Des lais pensai k'oï aveie'* ('I thought of the lays which I had heard', v. 33); *'Plusurs en ai oï conter'* ('I have heard a number of them told', v. 39). The creative process behind these twelve short compositions seems to be envisaged as follows. An *aventure* occurs in the life of one or more individuals, a special event or period, unexpected but often apparently preordained. The *aventure* was recounted and became known. It was heard by the Bretons who composed a lay about it – a short lyrical composition sung to the accompaniment of an instrument such as a harp or rote (see *Guigemar*, vv. 883–6). The author in turn relates (the verbs are *dire* and *conter*) the *aventure*, the *lai*, the *aventure* of the *lai* or the truth of the *lai*. It has been argued on the basis of expressions such as *'conter les contes'* (*Guigemar*, vv. 19–21) and *'dire le conte'* (*Eliduc*, vv. 1–3) that these new compositions should be entitled *contes* ('tales'). But the verb *conter* and the concept of the *conte* seem to relate to the entire process by which the *aventure* is rescued from oblivion and transformed into a Breton lay or a short story in French. The new poems can equally well be regarded as lays: *'Quant de lais faire m'entremet'* ('When I undertake to compose lays', *Bisclavret*, v. 1); *'Puis que des lais ai comencé'* ('Now that I have begun to compose lays', *Yonec*, v. 1).

Who is this author who sprinkles the prologues and epilogues so liberally with verbs in the first person and even intervenes on occasion to make comments within the tales? The sole indication concerning an author for the collection of poems in the Harley manuscript occurs at the beginning of what is normally regarded as the prologue to *Guigemar*:

> *Oëz, seignurs, ke dit Marie,*
> *Ki en sun tens pas ne s'oblie.* [3–4]

'Hear, lords, the words of Marie who in her time does not neglect her obligations.' Marie is anxious to make herself known to her audience and to stress that she does not intend to squander her talents. The somewhat obscure phrase *'en sun tens'* ('in her time') may mean little more than 'now' ('now that she has the opportunity, in her turn'), but there is probably an element of continuity envisaged, a link between the twelfth-century author and the ancient writers mentioned in the Prologue (the *philesophe*, v. 17, or the Bretons who first composed and disseminated the lays). Armed with excellent material ('He who treats of good material', *Guigemar*, v. 1) and endowed with the gift of knowledge and eloquence ('He to whom God has given knowledge and eloquence of speech', Prologue, vv. 1–2), Marie is determined not to be bullied into abandoning her work because of malicious gossip and aggressive behaviour (see *Guigemar*, vv. 5–18). We do not know at precisely what moment in her career Marie wrote the prologue to *Guigemar*, but it is clear that, when she did, her work was sufficiently well known for it to have aroused jealousy and perhaps for it to have been the object of plagiarism. It has been suggested that Marie was cross that her lay of *Lanval* had been used by the author of *Graelent*.* Whatever the background to Marie's remarks, we have the strong impression of dealing with an author proud of her reputation (*pris*) and of her literary talents.

The fact that only *Guigemar* of the twelve lays contains an allusion to an author provides at least some justification for the view that the twelve stories were not necessarily written by the same author. The vagaries of scribal practice and the uncertainty of manuscript transmission even make possible the extreme view that the name Marie was added by a scribe (the Harley manuscript

---

* Julian Harris, *Marie de France: the Lays Guigemar, Lanval and a Fragment of Yonec, with a Study of the Life and Work of the Author* (New York: Columbia University, 1930), p. 9.

seems to date from between fifty and eighty years after the composition of the lays) and that our author might even have been a man. The indisputably awkward link between the general Prologue and the curious two-part prologue to *Guigemar* (followed by the lengthy prologue to *Equitan*) certainly raises important questions concerning the authorship of the twelve lays, the order of composition and the nature of the collection.

However, over the years (the *Lais* were first published in 1819) most readers will have felt that they were reading a group of stories by one author. Few will have been convinced that the poems were written in the order found in Harley and likewise few will have attributed an equal degree of literary merit to each of the tales. *Equitan* lacks the subtlety of *Guigemar* or *Lanval*. *Laüstic* and *Chevrefoil* have a poetic intensity missing from *Chaitivel*. The question of whether the twelve poems were written by a woman is more delicate. One can point to such details as the author's evident interest in the welfare of infants (*Le Fresne* and *Milun*) and to the central role played in the structure of the tales by the sexual frustration of young women who had been married off to older men because of their child-rearing capabilities (see *Guigemar*, *Yonec*, *Laüstic*, *Milun* and *Chevrefoil*). It would come as no surprise if we were to learn one day that the author of the *Lais* had known such unhappiness and that she had experienced loneliness in a foreign country (see *Lanval*, vv. 35–8). In general the heroines of the lays are likeable and resourceful creatures. In spite of the risks they are forced to run, they contrive to see their lovers at regular intervals. In *Laüstic* it is the lady who gives a new direction to the story by calling upon the nightingale to act as an excuse for her nocturnal rendez-vous, and it is she who hits on the idea of sending the corpse to her lover. In *Milun* the young girl masterminds the plan whereby her baby is spirited away to her sister in Northumbria, and it is the young man's beloved in the *Deus Amanz* who proposes that he should make the trip to Salerno in search of a strength-giving potion. None of these factors is conclusive as a sign of the femininity of the author. But one wonders whether a male author would have written the words we find in the prologue to *Guigemar*: 'But when there is in a country a man *or a woman* of great reputation, those who are jealous of his or her talents (*sun bien*) often say spiteful things' (vv. 7–10).

If we are still tempted to say that a single reference to an author called Marie, in not far off 6,000 lines of text, is insufficient evidence of authorship or even of her existence, we can take heart from the remarks of a contemporary of Marie, Denis Piramus, who wrote, around 1180, a didactic poem entitled *The Life of St Edmund the King*.* In his lengthy prologue Denis tells us that his poem was written as a mark of repentance for a youth devoted to folly and sin. He had had ample experience of court life and with his courtly cronies composed a variety of love songs. Now his energies were to be turned towards an edifying work which would have the advantage of being true. As such it would contrast markedly with the poems of some of his contemporaries. He cites the author of the long romance *Partonopeu de Blois*, whose skill he praises and to whose popularity in aristocratic courts he attests. But his work, says Denis, is nothing more than '*fable*', '*menceonge*' or '*sounge*', a pack of lies, fictitious nonsense. He goes on to quote the case of Dame Marie, who composed '*les vers de lais,/Ke ne sunt pas del tut verais*' ('lays in verse which are not at all true', vv. 37–8). Marie's poetry has caused great praise to be heaped on her and it is much appreciated by counts and barons and knights who love to have her writings read out again and again. Moreover, it is not only the male members of the court who take pleasure in the lays. Denis adds that 'the lays are accustomed to please the ladies: they listen to them joyfully and willingly, for they are just what they desire'.

One could scarcely ask for clearer confirmation on a number of key issues. There was a lady by the name of Marie who wrote lays. These lays were immensely popular with men and women in aristocratic circles. Evidently Marie's work caught the imagination of her age, in the sense both of reflecting its ideals and of satisfying its desire for entertainment. As Denis Piramus is associated only with England, we can assume that Marie was known in English courts. She is known to Denis by name, whereas he mentions merely 'the man who composed *Partonopeu*'. We can see too that her poems were regarded by her contemporaries as *lais* (v. 37, v. 46). But, if Denis Piramus's evidence confirms that Marie's lays were circulating in British courts, probably during the 1170s and

* Denis Piramus, *La Vie seint Edmund le Rei, poème anglo-normand du XII*ᵉ* siècle*, ed. H. Kjellman (Göteborg: Wettergren and Kerber, 1935; reprint Geneva: Slatkine, 1974).

1180s, we cannot thereby be certain that she wrote all the poems in the Harley collection. On this point it would be wise to look carefully at her prologues.

Five of the prologues indicate that the lay in question is not an isolated composition: *Guigemar*, vv. 19–21, 'I shall tell you very briefly the tales which I know to be true, from which the Bretons composed the lays'; *Bisclavret*, v. 1, 'When I undertake to compose lays'; *Lanval*, vv. 1–2, 'I shall tell you the story of another lay, as it happened'; *Yonec*, v. 1, vv. 3–4, 'Now that I have begun the lays ... I shall relate in rhyme the stories I know concerning them'; *Milun*, vv. 1–2, 'Anyone who intends to tell a new (or different) story must begin in a new (or different) way'. To this one can add the prologue to *Equitan*, which uses the expression *'fere les lais'* ('to compose the lays', v. 7) and which is clearly meant to introduce a number of poems, and the general Prologue, which speaks of the lays which Marie had heard. The general Prologue has at least three aims. It is autobiographical in that it relates the reason why Marie selected the lays, how and why they came to be written, and the means by which they had come to her attention. It is also literary and exegetical. The Prologue opens with stress on the responsibility of the gifted, a discussion of the working habits of some of Marie's predecessors and of the process of assimilation and interpretation, and with a comment on the value of study and of undertaking a demanding project.

The final fourteen lines of the Prologue represent a third aim, a dedication, in direct speech, to a 'noble king'. Of the two possible candidates, Henry II and his son Henri au Cort Mantel, the former is the more likely. The Young King, crowned in 1170, may perhaps have merited the epithets *pruz* ('worthy') and *curteis* ('courtly') more than his father, but Henry II was a cultured man and he is known to have had contact with contemporary poets such as Wace and Benoît de Sainte-Maure. Henry II was always the true king and he never invested any real authority in his sons. Hence their revolt in 1173. But, whichever king Marie had in mind, it was for the English court and for the Plantagenets that she 'undertook to assemble the lays' (*'M'entremis des lais assembler'*, Prologue, v. 47). The verb *assembler* can be seen as designating the process by which each lay is put together from its constituent parts, the bringing together of the various lays in the collection now being offered to the noble king, and the careful constitution of a unified, well-balanced group of stories. The end-product is the result of a strong sense of responsibility, literary ambitions, and a good deal of burning of the midnight candle: *'Soventes fiez en ai veillié'* ('I have often stayed awake at night working on them', Prologue, v. 42).

In what order were the lays composed? This is a question to which there can be no definitive answer. Some readers have felt that *Guigemar*, the first lay in the collection, was the first one to have been composed by Marie. It has been argued that *Equitan* and *Chaitivel* were Marie's last lays, written after she had become acquainted with the Provençal code of love. Given the precise date of the *Roman de Brut* of Wace (1155) and accepting the tentative date of the *Roman de Thèbes* as 1150–55 and the *Roman d'Eneas* as 1160–65, it is possible to envisage some lays, such as the *Deus Amanz* and *Lanval*, as having been composed under the influence of the *Brut* and the *Thèbes*, and others, such as *Guigemar*, *Eliduc* and *Milun*, as having been influenced by these two texts, but also by the *Eneas*. Other lays, such as *Bisclavret*, *Laüstic* and *Le Fresne*, do not appear to show any specific borrowings from the three texts and could perhaps have been composed in the early 1150s. Another promising line of inquiry is the question of the geographical references in the poems. *Equitan*, *Le Fresne*, *Bisclavret*, the *Deus Amanz*, *Laüstic* and *Chaitivel* are or appear to be set fundamentally in Brittany or Normandy. There are no sea journeys in these lays and, apart from the young man's visit to Salerno in the *Deus Amanz*, not much movement. These lays could well have been written in France.

Guigemar and Eliduc begin their adventures in Brittany and then leave Brittany by sea. Eliduc sails to Devon. We are not told where Guigemar lands, but Marie could have had in mind for him a destination in South Wales or south-west England. Milun, born in South Wales, is a keen traveller. At the outset of the text he is known in Ireland, Norway, Gotland, England and Scotland. His beloved is married off to a local baron while he is away in search of *pris* ('fame') as a mercenary. In the closing stages of the text he travels to Normandy and Brittany in pursuit of tournaments, and his son, on deciding that he must seek greater *pris* than his father, travels from his home in Northumbria to Southampton, where he catches a boat for Barfleur, near Cherbourg, a common route from England to France. He too heads for the tournaments of Brittany. The town of Caerleon in Gwent is mentioned in *Milun* and this town reappears in *Yonec*, which also mentions Caerwent, a few miles away. *Lanval* is set in Carlisle, *Eliduc* contains references to Totnes and Exeter, and *Chevrefoil*, set in Cornwall, mentions Tintagel. Like Milun, Tristram was born in South Wales. Thus everything suggests that when writing the lays in this group Marie herself had travelled. She had perhaps settled in Britain, having left France as a result of marriage or in the furtherance of her professional career. Adding the criterion of literary merit, one can argue that *Equitan*, *Chaitivel* and *Bisclavret*, despite being interesting stories and illustrating several themes common to the entire collection, are less well written than the other lays and may have been composed before them. The prologue to *Equitan* could well have been intended originally as the introduction to the new genre and the new undertaking on which Marie was embarking. The Harley collection, which was not necessarily the first collection to be established by Marie, was probably prepared after she had lived in Britain for a few years. It must have been presented to the Plantagenet court no later than the 1180s. Henry II died in 1189, the Young King in 1183. There is no discernible influence in the *Lais* from Chrétien de Troyes, which might suggest that the collection was offered as early as the 1160s, before the murder of Becket and the deterioration in Henry's domestic life. In arranging her lays Marie may have deliberately placed a longer lay, containing a positive illustration of the power of love and the importance of fidelity, before a shorter composition depicting the painful, tragic consequences of love and foolish or vicious behaviour. In the case of *Chevrefoil* and *Eliduc* this process was reversed in order to provide a fitting conclusion for the collection. Marie may also have had mathematical considerations in mind, to ensure that a pair of lays could be recited at one sitting.

None of this conflicts with perhaps our most precious piece of information concerning our author. The Harley manuscript, as has been mentioned, contains a collection of fables. In all, these fables occur in no less than twenty-three manuscripts. At the beginning of the Epilogue the author writes:

Al finement de cest escrit,
Qu'en Romanz ai traitié e dit,
Me numerai pur remembrance:
Marie ai num, si sui de France. [1–4]

'At the close of this text, which I have written and composed in French, I shall name myself for posterity: my name is Marie and I come from France.' The expression *'pur remembrance'* ('for posterity') is one we encounter in the Prologue to the *Lais* (v. 35), in the prologue to *Equitan* (v. 7) and in the epilogue to *Bisclavret* (v. 318). Marie adds, in the Epilogue to the *Fables*, 'The writer who forgets himself is a poor workman' (*'Cil uevre mal ki sei ublie'*, v. 8), using the verb *sei oblier*, which is also associated with her naming of herself in the prologue to *Guigemar*. Thus the belief that the author of the *Fables* and the author of the *Lais* are one and the same person is one which almost all readers have been willing to embrace. The morals of the fables, although more practical than any lessons to be drawn from the lays, do not conflict with the overall vision of the world depicted therein.

The collection of fables was translated from English: *'M'entremis de cest livre faire | E de l'Engleis en Romanz traire'* ('I undertook to write this book and to translate the English into French', Epilogue, vv. 11–12). One notes the use of the verb *entremetre* ('to undertake, begin'), which is also found in the Prologue to the *Lais* (vv. 32, 47). The translation of the fables from English could have been started or even completed before the Harley collection was finalized and one can assume that the task was executed in England. Marie tells us that the *Fables* were commissioned by a certain Count William, so a further assumption is that Marie was sufficiently well known as a poet to warrant his faith in her abilities. Marie's Count is the most valiant man in the kingdom (Epilogue, v. 10), the flower of chivalry, learning and courtliness (Prologue, vv. 31–2), and a man with an eye for the potential of a literary form seemingly unknown in French. The question of which Count William Marie was alluding to has exercised the minds of many a scholar. During the second part of the twelfth century Count Williams were not in short supply. Tempting identifications have been made. If the *Fables* were composed during the reign of Henry II, William of Mandeville is a distinct possibility. Earl of Essex from 1167 to 1175, he was on excellent terms with the king. Sydney Painter has pointed out that in the Pipe Rolls for 1167–75, which indicate debts to the king, William of Mandeville was the only nobleman to be designated as Earl William, and in the *Bible* of Guiot de Provins (v. 388) he is listed as a literary patron.* He died in 1189. But also plausible for the early period is William of Gloucester (d. 1183), a boyhood friend of Henry II. This William was the son of Robert of Gloucester, illegitimate son of Henry II's grandfather, Henry I. Robert was a scholar himself and a protector of writers such as William of Malmesbury and Geoffrey of Monmouth, whom he inspired to write the *Historia Regum Britanniae*. Henry II was educated in his house, and on his death in 1147 his son inherited his extensive lands and his great library. William of Gloucester was an influential knight who supported Henry against the rebellious barons.

For the period after the death of Henry II in 1189 a good candidate is William Longsword (born *c.* 1150), illegitimate son of Henry II and Rosamond Clifford. He became Earl of Salisbury in 1196 and the epitaph on his tomb, *flos comitum Willelmus* ('William, flower of counts'), recalls Marie's *'Ki flurs est de chevalerie'* ('Who is the flower of chivalry', Prologue, v. 31). An even better contender perhaps is William Marshal, preceptor of the Young King and Regent of England from 1216 to 1219. William Marshal acquired the Earldom of Striguil and Pembroke in 1189 and his military skills and chivalric reputation were second to none. The lays of *Guigemar*, *Milun* and *Eliduc* portray knights whose ideals were actually realized by William, who single-handedly raised the standards of British knighthood. R. W. Southern points out that British knights 'were looked on as easy game by the tougher knights of France until the professionalism of William Marshal gave them a reputation for military competence'.†

Until the later eighteenth century Marie de France was regarded simply as the author of the *Fables*. Moreover, she was considered as a thirteenth-century writer and the allusion to Count William was envisaged as applying to a French count such as Guillaume de

---

* *Les Œuvres de Guiot de Provins, poète lyrique et satirique*, ed. J. Orr (Manchester: Imprimerie de l'Université, 1915), p. 21.

† R. W. Southern, *Medieval Humanism and other Essays* (Oxford: Blackwell, 1970), p. 143.

Dampierre (d. 1251), Count of Flanders. For most early scholars the 'noble king' was Henry III of France. It was only in the last decades of the nineteenth century, thanks principally to the work of Karl Warnke, who edited the *Lais* (1885) and the *Fables* (1898), that Marie was placed firmly in the second half of the twelfth century. Warnke thought that Marie's language differed little from that of Wace, and if this view is allied to Ernest Hoepffner's conviction that she was considerably influenced by the *Roman de Brut* an early date is likely both for the *Lais* and the *Fables*. There is no reason to rule out the possibility that the *Fables* were begun before the composition of the later lays. The *Fables* could well have been dedicated to William of Mandeville or William of Gloucester, both friends of Henry II, perhaps in the 1170s. An earlier date than many scholars have assumed is also possible for the third work to be attributed commonly to Marie de France, the *Espurgatoire seint Patriz*. This 2,300-line account of the knight Owein's descent into the Otherworld via a cavern on Station Island in Lough Derg (County Donegal) is based on the *Tractatus de Purgatorio Sancti Patricii*, written confusingly by a monk H. (either Henry or Hugh) of Sawtry (Saltry) and dedicated, even more confusingly, to abbot H. de Sartis. Abbot H. has often been identified as Henry, abbot of Old Wardon in Bedfordshire during the few years preceding 1215, which would be the approximate date of the *Tractatus*. But it is far more likely that the text was dedicated to Hugh, abbot from 1173 to 1185/6. Thus the *Tractatus* would have been written during this period, and the version by Marie ('*Jo, Marie, ai mis, en memoire, | Le livre de l'Espurgatoire*', 'I, Marie, have recorded for posterity the book dealing with the Purgatory', vv. 2297–8, ed. Warnke) could have been composed around 1180, certainly no later than the early 1190s.

Who was this versatile author, the first woman of her times to have written successfully in the vernacular? She was definitely not Marie de Champagne, daughter of Eleanor of Aquitaine and patroness of Chrétien de Troyes, as Winkler suggested. A tempting, but by no means fully convincing, identification is with Marie, abbess of Shaftesbury in Dorset, illegitimate daughter of Geoffrey Plantagenet and half-sister to Henry II. A fragment of an Anglo-Norman version of the *Espurgatoire* legend has been found on the cover of a twelfth-century psalter belonging to the abbey at

Shaftesbury (but not Marie de France's version). One of the benefactors of the abbey was William Longsword, who gave lands to it and lent his name as a witness to a confirmation charter dating from 1198. Mary is attested as abbess in 1181 and still in 1215. The founder of the abbey was King Alfred, to whom Marie de France attributes the translation into English of the Latin collection of fables forming the basis of her own work (*Fables*, Epilogue, vv. 16–17).

A claim has been made, albeit somewhat thin, for Mary, abbess of Reading. This abbey was well known as a centre of literary activity and had in its possession the Harley manuscript containing, as we have seen, both the *Fables* and the *Lais*. There is no clear-cut reason why either work could not have been written by an abbess or a nun, and there is some slight evidence of experience of monastic life in *Le Fresne, Yonec* and *Eliduc*. But the prominence of the motif of adultery in the *Lais* (see also fables 44 and 45), Marie's attitude towards the dissolution of marriage in *Le Fresne* and *Eliduc*, and her evident interest in the chivalric life suggest that these love poems were not written by someone steeped in ecclesiastical ideology. Tournaments were forbidden by the Church and a Christian burial was denied to those killed in them, but Marie was obviously a keen spectator at such events and the three fallen knights in *Chaitivel* are buried with great honour.

Marie de France was certainly an educated lady of good family, who knew Latin well enough to have contemplated translating a Latin work into French (*Lais*, Prologue, vv. 28–32) and to have done so in the case of the *Espurgatoire*. She was obviously a good linguist and acquired a sound knowledge of English before translating the fables. She was also fully conversant with the life and aspirations of the nobility of her time. Her education could well have been obtained in a convent and her knowledge of court life from her upbringing and personal experiences in England. Was she Marie, the eighth child of Waleran de Meulan (also called Waleran de Beaumont), a member of one of the greatest of the Norman houses? Waleran's fief was in the French Vexin, which would tally with Marie's statement that she comes from France and explain her evident local knowledge of the town of Pitres in the Norman Vexin (see the *Deus Amanz*, vv. 11–20). Marie de Meulan married Hugh Talbot, baron of Cleuville, owner of lands in Herefordshire and Buckinghamshire, as well as in Normandy, and a member of a family prominent in several English counties including Devonshire, Gloucestershire and Kent. Marie's father is an interesting figure – a loyal and courageous soldier, but also a well-educated man who may have written Latin verse. Moreover, several of the manuscripts of the *Historia Regum Britanniae* of Geoffrey of Monmouth are dedicated to him. It is tempting to think that his daughter may have known William of Gloucester, a possible Count William, as his father was also one of Geoffrey's dedicatees. Marie de Meulan may, however, have been too young to be Marie de France, as her birth seems to date from the 1140s, perhaps as late as 1150.

The most recent identification has been as Marie, countess of Boulogne after 1154, daughter of Stephen of Blois (King of England, 1135–54) and of Matilda of Boulogne. Educated in a convent, Marie de Boulogne became abbess of Romsey in Hampshire, but was removed from her convent by Henry II, who wanted to keep Boulogne in his sway. She was married off to Matthew of Flanders and thus became the sister-in-law of Hervé II, son of Guiomar of Léon (see *Guigemar*, vv. 27–37). Eventually, at some time between 1168 and 1180, Marie de Boulogne returned to a convent, perhaps that of Sainte Austreberthe at Montreuil-sur-Mer in her own county. Her Count William could have been William of Mandeville, a crusade companion of Philip of Flanders, her husband's brother. The 'noble king' would probably have been the Young King, as Philip and Matthew, originally supporters of Henry II, changed sides in 1173. Marie herself may have already been a supporter of the Young King, as in 1168 she sent Louis clandestine information about the secret negotiations between Henry and the Emperor Frederick.

But in spite of these intriguing efforts at determining her identity, Dame Marie remains something of a mystery. By far the most impressive piece of documentation we have, of course, is the text of the poems themselves. Here we have our principal guide to Marie's world and to her way of thinking. First, however, the poems in the present volume need to be situated in the wider context of twelfth-century French literature.

The second half of the twelfth century was in France a period of intense literary activity. *Chansons de geste* (long epic poems about heroes such as Charlemagne and Roland), romances of antiquity (Greek and Roman subject-matter), Arthurian romances, notably those by Chrétien de Troyes, love-lyrics of the *troubadours* in the South and the *trouvères* in the North, drama, both religious and secular, chronicles, saints' lives, a vast body of religious and didactic works – all of these were produced in a vernacular on a scale unknown before in Western Europe. Only the Old Germanic and Celtic peoples produced any literature of note before this date. Old French is the germinal literature in the Europe of the period, and the literary traffic is practically one-way, from France to England, Germany, the Low Countries, Scandinavia, the Iberian peninsula and Italy. This situation remains essentially unchanged until the rise of Italian literature in the age of Dante, Boccaccio and Petrarch. In fields other than literature, too, the period is one of outstanding innovation and creativity, and one thinks in particular of theology (St Bernard) and of philosophy (Abelard, Bernard Sylvester, Alan of Lille). The building of some of the great cathedrals and the founding of some of the great universities also rank amongst the major achievements of the twelfth century.

As a result of the Norman invasion, political, cultural and personal interchange between the continent and England increased enormously, and the insular dialect of French known as Anglo-Norman became the language of culture in England. Not only were continental works copied by Anglo-Norman scribes, but much literature was also produced by English authors writing originally in Anglo-Norman. It hardly needs pointing out again that the context of Marie's work is at least partly an English one, for whoever she was exactly, she was certainly a woman of French descent and upbringing living and working in England. Her personal circumstances as a Frenchwoman in England and her almost certainly religious education would have exposed her to a wide variety of formative influences. Her evident knowledge of Old French and Anglo-Norman literature is supplemented by the interest she seems to have taken in the orally circulating tales of her day which she frequently claims as the source of the *Lais*.

The aim of the rest of this introduction is to look at Marie's *Lais* in relation to the literature of the period in general and to show what features the *Lais* share with other kinds of works and to suggest what aspects of her poems are characteristic of the *lai* in particular. Although comparison of the *lai* with epic, chronicle, drama, hagiography and religious literature in general is not without point, the most fruitful directions for investigation would seem to be comparison with other narrative genres of love and chivalry, and the lyric, all of which share some features of subject-matter and form with the *lai*.

Although Latin literature still predominates at the end of the twelfth century, as indeed it does throughout the Middle Ages, the use of the vernacular for such genres as the saint's life is a new and significant departure, implying as it does the desire to bring literature and learning within the reach of those with no knowledge of Latin: the *Vie de saint Alexis*, the *Voyage de saint Brendan*, and the *Vie de saint Thomas Becket* (by Guernes de Pont-Saint-Maxence) may be cited as examples. Other kinds of religious literature, such as sermons and similar didactic works, also began to flourish at more or less this time. Much of this literature is derived directly or indirectly from the Bible. Scientific literature appeared in the vernacular, too: bestiaries, lapidaries, lunaries, encyclopedic treatises, and so on. All of these works, then, available earlier only in Latin, began to be translated into, or composed directly in, the vernacular, both on the Continent and in Norman Britain. Other forms of vernacular literature, such as the *chanson de geste*, were written directly into Old French, and had never existed in large quantities, if at all, in Latin. The *chanson de geste* is the first of all the original Old French genres to flourish, and some believe that its popularity was waning when Marie wrote. This is difficult to prove, but *chansons de geste* were being copied and revised (if not composed) in Marie's day and considerably later. The love-lyric first blossoms in Provence in Provençal in the eleventh and twelfth centuries, and migrates north with much of southern culture in the middle of the twelfth century. Marie is therefore working at a time when this sort of lyric is at the height of its popularity. The second half of the twelfth century also witnesses the all-important development of the romance, starting with the so-called romances of antiquity, the *Roman d'Eneas*, the *Roman de Thèbes*, and the *Roman de Troie*, Old French adaptations of Virgil's *Aeneid*, Statius's *Thebaid* and a Late Latin Troy narrative respectively. What is important to note here is that these texts graft a layer of courtly veneer on to the originals, particularly visible in the development of the love interest. This is either greatly expanded from hints in the original or often added afresh. Although it is impossible to name all other romances of this period, special mention ought to be made of the *Tristan* texts, the romances of Hue de Rotelande, and those of Chrétien de Troyes. These are all fully-fledged romances (unfortunately the Old French *Tristan* romances of Béroul and Thomas are both fragmentary) that count as classic models of the genre when compared with the transitional romances of antiquity. This is the vernacular context of the *Lais* of Marie de France.

In addition to the translation of the *Espurgatoire* there is further evidence of Marie's knowledge of Latin in her statement in the Prologue to the *Lais* that she had considered translating a Latin text before deciding to base her work on Breton tales. Nor is there any reason to doubt her claim in the *Fables* that she translated them from the English; her use of the occasional English word in the *Lais* also confirms this. Moreover she is well aware of the Greek fable tradition of Aesop and that of the Latin grammarians. A number of passages in the *Lais* in particular show the influence of Ovid's *Remedia Amoris* and *Metamorphoses*, two of the most widely read Latin texts of the Middle Ages. Classical literature in the Middle Ages, as we have already mentioned, was also known from vernacular translations and adaptations, and one text in particular can be shown to have influenced Marie in the *Lais*, namely the *Roman d'Eneas*, one of the romances of antiquity. The influence is especially apparent in the way in which Marie describes the growth of love and analyses the feelings of the characters, and although one cannot point to specific passages in the *Eneas* which have left their mark on Marie, she is clearly working in the same tradition in this respect. A case can also be made for her knowledge of the other two major romances of antiquity, the *Roman de Thèbes* and the *Roman de Troie*, although this is less convincing than the case of the *Eneas*.

With respect to her knowledge of other vernacular literature, it is equally difficult to show particular borrowings, but there are a number of works of which few scholars would now doubt the influence on Marie. While the *lai* as a genre has little to do with the chronicle, it is almost certain that Marie took a number of geographical names from the tradition of the *Bruts*, those British pseudo-histories of which the first is the *Historia Regum Britanniae* by Geoffrey of Monmouth (*c.* 1135). Marie seems to have known Gaimar's *Estoire des Engleis* and especially Wace's *Brut* (*c.* 1155), which she uses to create an archaic ambiance for the setting of the *Lais*. The *Chevrefoil* reveals not only a knowledge of the episode related in it, but also of the tradition of the Tristan legend in general, which existed in a number of variant, sometimes conflicting versions in the period Marie was writing the *Lais*. While the usefulness of source-hunting can be called into question, it is important for an understanding of Marie's work to realize that she was immersed in the classical and vernacular literature circulating during her lifetime, and that she is part of the mainstream of medieval culture, not a quaint oddity, however unique her work may be.

If the *Lais* and their author lie fairly and squarely in the mainstream of Old French vernacular literary production, what is the precise relationship of the *Lais* to other literary genres being produced at the time? With respect to the *chanson de geste*, the Old French heroic epic, it may be said that the contrast with the *lai* is almost total, in form, intention and spirit: the *chansons de geste*, written in assonating *laisses*, are intended to inspire the listener with pride and admiration for the deeds of the hero, and are imbued with a militant crusading spirit. One of the few points of contact between Marie's *Lais* and the epic is the express conviction that God is on the side of the virtuous characters and that he will punish the wicked. In so far as chronicle literature of the time shares some of these epic features, it stands in a similar relation to the *lai*, but is frequently cast in the same medium, that is to say the octosyllabic rhyming couplet. This last feature also links the *lai* to much didactic literature and the saint's life. To what extent the *lai* can be compared to these last two genres in respect of moral intention is difficult to say, given the fact that most medieval literature can be shown to contain some kind of lesson, explicit or implicit. Of the *lai* and the saint's life it might also be said that they both frequently revolve around a crisis in the life of the central figures, although the time-span of the actions of a saint's life is nearly always greater than that of the *lai*. In hagiography, divine intervention can play a similar role to the supernatural of the *lai*. By and large, however, it is the contrast between these genres and the *lai* that strikes the modern reader of medieval literature. The medieval conception of genres may not have led the listener of the time to see such differences, although he would almost certainly have been aware that he was dealing with various sorts of literature.

One basic distinction that can be made between the *lai* and the other Old French genres discussed so far which may well be at the root of the differences is that scholars generally regard the *lais* as belonging to what is known as 'courtly' literature and the epic and religious–didactic literature not. Now while generalizations such as this are quite properly open to modification and refinement, it can serve to explain why the *lais* resemble certain kinds of poem and not others. The term 'courtly' and its equivalents in other languages (*'courtois'*, *'höfisch'*, etc.), when used to describe certain sorts of literature, is a complex one and often misunderstood. Too loose and frequent use of the word by scholars is at least partly to blame. Basically, 'courtly' can have several meanings: a literal one of 'associated with a court' or extended ones of 'possessing characteristics of a type of literature intended for audiences at court' or 'showing characters whose actions are governed by a code of behaviour called "courtesy" '. The problem is further compounded by slack and indiscriminate use of the term 'courtly love' and the associations given it by C. S. Lewis. Yet, despite these problems, it is precisely the love-element that links the *lai* as a courtly genre to other forms of courtly literature such as the love-lyric and the romance.

We have already said that by the time Marie was writing the *Lais* there was already a well-established tradition of the love-lyric in France, especially in Provence. As a result of political developments and particularly as a result of the marriage of Eleanor of Aquitaine to Henry II in 1152, the culture of the southern courts moved northwards. The kind of 'courtly love' which characterizes the Provençal lyric is found again in the north, in lyric and narrative verse, albeit in a slightly different form. The love is always between persons of an exalted social status, often adulterous (a young wife closely guarded by a jealous old husband), nearly always problematic in some way or another, always profound and always refined. Despite having a cerebral appearance due to an extreme formalism, the love is not platonic, the physical union being discreetly alluded to as the ultimate goal for the sake of effect rather than out of prudishness. The *lai* resembles the lyric in that the love depicted is of an extreme intensity; the time-span of the *lai* is short, and although not quite as short as the moment of lyric passion, the effect of heightening the emotion is comparable. The longer the text and the longer the time-span covered by the events, the less concentrated the emotions depicted are likely to be.

To say that the audience of the *Lais* would have recognized the spring-time opening of *Yonec* or the jealous old husband motif of *Guigemar* as lyric elements is probably less accurate than saying that such features formed part of a stock of themes and motifs that a medieval poet had at his disposition and upon which he could draw when appropriate. It is important to point out here that the use of familiar material was not regarded in any way as second-rate or plagiaristic in the Middle Ages, rather that it conferred authority on the work, which was thereby sanctioned by it. This is true for both the basic material of many medieval works (in this case the Breton stories Marie claims she used) and the more incidental themes and motifs and stylistic devices such as those mentioned above. This is a fundamental concept which often proves to be a stumbling-block for the modern reader of medieval literature, accustomed as he is to the esteem in which originality is held. The medieval idea of literary creation was really one of re-creation in which existing material was reworked and elaborated on until something new was produced. Needless to say, poor poets are capable of producing poor poetry at any period. Having said all this, it must be admitted that the modern reader is less likely to react unfavourably to Marie's *Lais* than other medieval works of less immediate access.

Although most medieval vernacular verse was intended for recitation aloud rather than quiet reading, the *lai* has a particular connection with the lyric in so far as it is traditionally associated with a musical performance. Marie's *Lais*, however, are not apparently intended to be sung, and represent a more literary stage in the development of the genre. Nevertheless the musical history and lyric intensity of the *lai* must have been recognized by medieval audiences. That the musical connection was never forgotten is shown by the development of the so-called *lai lyrique* in the thirteenth and fourteenth centuries. These are often incorporated at particularly emotional moments in the Arthurian prose romances, often composed and sung by the characters within the romances themselves, to the accompaniment of a harp. Tristan is particularly well-known as a musician and author of *lais*, as witness Marie's own *Chevrefoil*.

If comparison between the *lai* and the lyric suggests itself because of brevity, intensity and a common concern with love as a subject-matter, the narrative nature of the *lai* sets it apart and invites comparison with other narrative genres, in particular the romance. Scholars have pointed out that the *lai* in some ways represents a transitional genre between the earlier Provençal love-lyrics, which provided later poets with a storehouse of themes and motifs, and the romance, which develops and transforms these themes and motifs at length. The *lai* is not the lyric expression of the poet-lover, desperate before his pitiless lady, nor the adventure-filled biography of the romance hero. The *lai*, as it were, takes its cue from the lyric in terms of the nature of the problem presented, and seems to illustrate this by concentrating on one particularly critical event or brief sequence of events in the life of the protagonists.

With the possible exception of *Eliduc*, it is an over-simplification to say that the *lai* treats briefly the matter of romance, as it is almost impossible to compress the narrative events of a full-length romance into the average *lai*. It is fairer to say that some *lais* relate an incident which it is possible to imagine being woven into a romance narrative, and by the same token there are episodes in romances which could be plucked out of context and stand on their own as *lais*. The first part of Chrétien de Troyes' *Erec et Enide*, for example, could function as an independent poem, although its integration into the romance as a whole gives it quite a different significance. In Marie's collection, *Chevrefoil* is again the obvious example of an episode that might form part of a longer Tristan narrative: some Tristan poems in fact *do* recount a similar event. Other *lais*, like *Lanval* and *Guigemar*, may be seen as concentrating on the initial and final events of a potentially longer narrative, which might have been fleshed out with many adventures and episodes into a romance. Another way of viewing the same phenomenon might be to say that the *lai* concentrates almost uniquely on the crisis which is at the same time the crux and core of the narrative. The *lai*, in fact, generally starts from a position of lack and crisis which is resolved into a period of happiness; the happiness is then confronted with a test which leads either to a satisfactory or an unsatisfactory resolution. The events of the *lai* are usually, as mentioned above, the decisive moments in the lives of the protagonists, and may lead to their living happily ever after or dying a tragic death.

Love as presented in the *Lais* seems a more spontaneous phenomenon than the love we frequently find in the romances, but this may be due again to the fundamental brevity of the genre, which precludes the kind of learned and rhetorical analysis of the sentiments that is characteristic of a good many courtly romances. The lovers in Marie's *Lais* are nearly always on their own and pitted against forces of evil in various forms: a jealous husband, an envious society and so on. It is in fact by virtue of their loving that the protagonists are set apart from the rest of society and privileged. Marie concentrates on the individuality of her characters and is not very concerned with their integration into society. If society does not appreciate the lovers, then the lovers die or abandon society, and society is the poorer for it. This stands in considerable contrast to the romances of Chrétien de Troyes, where one of the main concerns of the author is the (re-)integration of the lovers into society, in the (re-)establishing of a balance between love and chivalry and the reciprocal duties of individual and society.

With respect to the *idée reçue* of courtly love, characterized by the servant–mistress relationship of the lover and his lady, where the lady is worshipped, and which is often adulterous, the *Lais* illustrate the dangers inherent in generalizing. Some poems do have a timorous lover standing in fear of his lady, but the majority do not; some of Marie's relationships are adulterous, but others are not. In retrospect, it seems difficult to conceive why the ideas propounded by Gaston Paris and C. S. Lewis ever gained such general acceptance, unless it be that most readers of medieval literature read nothing but the stories of Lancelot and Guinevere and Tristan and Iseult. Classic as these stories may be, and their protagonists bywords for models of lovers, they are not in all respects typical of the kind of love-relationships portrayed in medieval literature. Love in medieval literature, as in any other period (indeed, in life itself), is too complex to be reduced to a single model which will not admit of variation. This is not to say that love in medieval literature, and in Marie's *Lais*, does not have characteristics specific to period or genre.

If we take the *Lais* as a whole work, compared with other works of medieval literature, the characteristic of Marie's view of love seems to be an almost inevitable association with suffering. Again, this is not to say that this is not typical of other sorts of literature, but given the brevity of the genre, the attention given to it by Marie leaves a stronger impression than it might have done in a longer and more diffuse treatment of similar material. If we now look at the *Lais* in more detail, we can see more clearly how their subject-matter is related to the early medieval view of love as a whole and how they reflect its many facets.

Lanval presents a problem of love-casuistry: the hero transgresses his lady's command not to reveal their love to anyone, but does so in order to preserve his life in the face of Guinevere's accusation. Is he guilty or not? and if so, of what? Such are the questions Marie seems to pose without providing explicit answers. The implied answer is that while Lanval should not have boasted of his love in the way he did, his lady retracts her over-rigorous condemnation of him by appearing at the trial to vindicate him. *Yonec* shows the classic situation of the *mal mariée* condemned to live without love. The plight of the lady is sufficient for Marie to justify her adultery with the hawk-knight. As in *Lanval*, it is a transgressed vow that causes the crisis: the lady forgets her lover's command to be discreet and moderate, for she calls upon him whenever she wishes and her radiant face reveals her secret. The idea of moderation (Old French *mesure*) is central to much of medieval literature and when present is the feature that keeps all other aspects of courtly and chivalric behaviour in equilibrium. The *dénouement* of that *lai*, like that of *Lanval*, leaves us in no doubt as to where Marie's sympathies lie.

Love also leads to the death of the lovers in three more *lais*. The choice of a Tristanian subject in *Chevrefoil* and the explicit statement at the beginning of the poem make the symbol of the intertwining plants one of the inevitable union of the lovers in death. The *Deus Amanz* shows again that lack of *mesure*, as in *Yonec*, leads to tragedy, but this time Marie gives another slant to the problem: the girl does her utmost to persuade her young beloved to drink his potion and one must ask oneself why he refuses to do so. Not simply out of love, but also out of vanity, out of a desire to be the first to be able to meet the father's requirements. The love in the *Deus Amanz* is tragic because, unlike in *Chevrefoil*, its mortal nature is not inevitable. The *mal mariée* also appears in another *lai*, *Laüstic*, where love leads to death. This time, however, the death is not that of either of the lovers, but that of the nightingale, symbol of the love. Yet the death of the nightingale does not symbolize the end of the love, only of the idyll, for the lady sends the heart of the bird to her lover precisely as a symbol of their eternal attachment.

Yonec, *Chevrefoil* and *Laüstic* all show extra-marital love, all incorporate the usual situation of the unmarried lover and the unhappily married lady, and in none of the three does Marie give an indication of disapproving of this state of affairs. In *Eliduc*, the situation is different and more delicate: here, an apparently happily married husband falls in love with another woman, and here, also, it is the woman who takes the unusual step of first declaring her love to the man. Marie has reversed the standard 'courtly love' situation and put quite a new perspective on the problems of extra-marital love, for Eliduc, however much he loves the king's daughter, does not forget the vows of fidelity he made to his wife. It is the revelation of his married state by the sailor that precipitates, but does not cause, the crisis, quickly solved by Guildelüc's readiness to take the veil and thus enables Eliduc and Guilliadun to enjoy their love with the blessing of society and God. Guildelüc's action is comparable to that of Fresne in *Le Fresne*, where the heroine even goes so far as to attend to the preparations of her beloved's wedding-night; in this case, her virtue is rewarded when her identity is revealed, and her social status and marriageability thereby established.

The theme of the *mal mariée* reappears in *Guigemar*, this time in combination with another motif found elsewhere in medieval literature, that of the man who spurns love and is then taken unawares by it. This time Marie shows that love, even adulterous love, if loyal and deep, need not necessarily lead to the death of the lovers. Inevitably, however, the love does lead to suffering before the lovers' single-minded fidelity leads to triumph and union. In a sense, *Guigemar* is one of Marie's more chivalric *lais*, as the love it portrays is associated with the trappings of romance such as abduction, tournament and single-combat. *Milun*, too, shows the rewards that devotion brings, for the twenty-year correspondence and only occasional meeting is crowned by the young man's discovery of Milun and subsequent union of his parents. This *lai* contains a number of themes and motifs met elsewhere: the woman falling in love with the man on the basis of his reputation alone, and the combat between father and son.

Bisclavret and *Equitan* have been linked in the past as the two *lais* of Marie which seem to condemn the idea of courtly love and adultery, but this is on closer inspection not so. They are linked, however, by a certain savagery in the *dénouement* and their condemnation of disloyalty. In *Bisclavret* the woman is punished for disloyalty to her husband and for robbing him of what human aspects he retains, thereby despoiling him of his reason; there is no question of the lady loving her neighbour, and Marie explicitly tells us that she does not. The two adulterers in *Equitan* do love each other, but again their savage end is not to be seen necessarily as a condemnation of adultery. Even though the king is aware of the immorality of loving his seneschal's wife, Marie does not insist on this. It is rather their communal plan to dispose of the lady's husband that is culpable in the eyes of the poetess.

Chaitivel is the one *lai* that really seems to belong to the casuistical tradition of Andreas Capellanus and the courts of love, for it presents us with a *quaestio amoris*: who is to be pitied most – the lady who has effectively lost all her four lovers in one day, or the one survivor who can see his lady but not enjoy her favours because of his infirmity? Once more, the association of love with suffering is evident, and once more the guilty party is punished, the lady being condemned to lose all her lovers because of her vanity in refusing to choose one of them. Her selfishness is also evident in the title she wants to give to the *lai* that she writes about her own misfortunes, *The Four Sorrows*; the unfortunate survivor realizes this and suggests in his turn that it should rather be called after him, *The Wretched One*.

Does an overall view of love emerge from this consideration of the *Lais*? This is hardly possible, since Marie seems to delight in telling us that each particular situation calls for the appropriate action and that, from a moral point of view, each case requires a separate evaluation. One needs to look no further for illustration than the approval or condemnation of adultery in the various *Lais*. As Emanuel Mickel has said: 'The suffering from what is often called love is present in every *lai*, but the means of overcoming this suffering is beautifully and subtly illustrated.'* Mickel has also aptly remarked that the truly important consideration for Marie always seems to be the quality of the love: in *Equitan*, *Bisclavret* and *Chaitivel*, cupidity leading to crime and disaster; in *Laüstic* and *Chevrefoil*, love of unfulfilment; in *Guigemar* and *Lanval*, love which overcomes obstacles; in the *Deus Amanz*, *Yonec* and *Milun*, the point is that the real significance of the union is fruition; finally, the charitable devotion of the heroines in *Eliduc* and *Le Fresne* shows that there is a more spiritual side to earthly love.

We have already touched on the relative brevity of the *lai* compared to the romance and seen how Marie chooses to relate brief but crucial moments from the lives of the protagonists, but it may be worthwhile looking at the narrative structure of the *Lais* in a little more detail. As we have already suggested, the length of the *Lais* tends to determine the kinds of adventures described and to some extent the structure of the poems. It is possible to make a distinction between the shorter *lais* (less than 500 lines: *Equitan*, *Bisclavret*, the *Deus Amanz*, *Laüstic*, *Chaitivel* and *Chevrefoil*), where it is the *dénouement* that is important, the medium-length ones (*Le Fresne*, *Lanval*, *Yonec* and *Milun*), where a situation of stability is quickly reached but temporarily endangered, and the longer ones (*Guigemar* and *Eliduc*), where the narrative has two distinct temporal movements. Although it is in some ways easy to see how the shorter *lais* could be expanded by stressing events that Marie merely mentions or leaves implicit, her narrative art is essentially one of economy. Only information that is necessary for an understanding of the story is included, and long periods of time are frequently passed over in silence. Here again, comparison with the romance is enlightening, for this is a genre which often takes as its subject the whole life of a hero or a detailed analysis of a particular period in his life.

The question of relationship to the romance can also be investigated via the use of the concept of adventure in the two genres. It is quite clear, given the frequent use of the word *aventure*

* Emanuel J. Mickel, Jr, *Marie de France* (New York: Twayne Publishers, 1974), p. 121.

in the *Lais*, that it is a key term for our understanding of the nature of narrative in the genre. The idea of *aventure* can perhaps best be looked at by means of its etymology. The word is derived from the Latin *advenire*, 'to happen' (literally, 'to come to'), and in Marie's *Lais*, as elsewhere, adventures are things which happen to people with no warning and which cannot be sought. There is a lack of awareness about the heroes of the *Lais* when compared with those of the romance, who actually seek adventures or go on quests. Marie's characters are usually shaken to the core (not necessarily in a negative way) by the adventures that overtake them and them alone, whereas the heroes of romance take adventures in their stride. The adventures in the *Lais* are events which usually bring about a fundamental change in the lives of the protagonists, whereas in romance they often serve to bring out potential or confirm and strengthen something already present. It has been mentioned in another connection that Marie is not concerned with showing her characters integrated into society, and, if anything, happiness seems possible only outside the normal world. It has also been pointed out in this respect that the adventures in the *Lais* never have beneficial effects on society and relate only to the individuals concerned, whereas adventures in romance often lead to the liberation of captives or ridding a land of evil customs. In the *Lais*, then, the adventures form the basis of the narrative structure, but the nature of the adventure is different from that in romance.

Marie is quite clearly aware of the kind of techniques romance writers had at their disposal, and in terms of pure narrative structure that is evident from, say, *Eliduc*. Most romance writers will use a tournament or feast or even the first appearance of a character as a means of expanding their narratives with long descriptions, but Marie uses only as much description as is necessary for the comprehension of the story. Occasionally she will give a longer description, such as that of the tent in *Lanval* or of the ship in *Guigemar*, but these are generally in order to stress a particularly important point. The effect of these descriptions in romance is usually to create a statelier tempo for the narrative; the lack of them in the *Lais* has the effect of reinforcing the timelessness also suggested by other means.

Something similar may be said about Marie's characterization.

While it is often fruitless to look for great psychological depth in characters from medieval literature in general – the equation of depths of characterization with great literature is a relatively modern one – it is even more fruitless in such a short genre as the *lai*. Marie does not give us penetrating insight into the minds of her characters. She does, however, use the popular romance devices of interior monologue or meditation and dialogue in a moderate way, though to nothing like the extent that Chrétien de Troyes does. Most of what we know about her characters we learn from their actions. While some of the central characters are drawn with a certain degree of refinement, Marie's protagonists are by and large types common to medieval literature: noble knights and ladies, some of them *mal mariées*, jealous old husbands, devoted wives, etc. The virtues and vices they possess are the stock ones of medieval characters: *mesure* or *démesure*, charity or cupidity, fidelity or infidelity, jealousy or acceptance, generosity or greed, etc. As has been noted the general impression received from the *Lais* is that the women characters are more forceful than the men.

Another element that links the *lai* to the romance is the supernatural. It is debatable to what extent this can be considered a generic question, however, as not all of the *Lais* or all romances contain marvels of this kind. Nevertheless, enough of Marie's *Lais* contain supernatural elements for the reader to be struck by their presence, and a word of comment may be in order. Three *lais*, *Guigemar*, *Lanval* and *Yonec*, have the main protagonist come into contact with the Otherworld, and in *Guigemar* and *Lanval* the hero is actually taken there. Yet the Otherworld is not necessarily a place where things happen that are inexplicable in terms of the laws of physics, but rather an ideal world where the hero achieves what he would wish to achieve in the ordinary world. There is nothing particularly supernatural about Lanval's fairy-mistress or especially Guigemar's *mal mariée*. The ship in *Guigemar* could equally well have been manned by sailors, and the swan in *Milun* is not necessarily supernatural and could for all practical purposes be replaced by a human messenger. The potion in the *Deus Amanz* is also a borderline case, and is certainly not the kind of love-potion drunk by Tristan and Iseult. Indeed, Marie specifically says where it came from and how the hero acquired it. *Bisclavret* is in a sense typical here: the lady's wicked behaviour is brought about by a supernatural phenomenon, but that phenomenon is in itself not stressed by Marie, whose interests lie in the injustice done a man by his wife. Irrespective, however, of whether the particular *lai* contains supernatural elements or not, it is incontestable that the world of the *lai* is a fairy-tale world where the unexpected can happen at any time without rational explanation The fact that Marie often chose folktale material for her *lais* is partly responsible for this, but even where there is no visible popular source, the atmosphere is similar to that of the fairy-tale. This also to some extent accounts for the individuality of the *Lais* as the poetic reality of the fairy-tale is a private not a public one. Lest the irreality of the *Lais* be overstressed, it should be pointed out that there is also more than the odd point of contact with medieval reality: not only are geographical names used, but the characters are medieval people, not the vague characters of the fairy-tale; none of the protagonists is immortal (except perhaps Lanval and his lady), and the harsh reality of death is often present; in *Bisclavret* and particularly in *Lanval* we are also aware of contact with the real legal system in operation at the time.

It is fair to assume that despite some differences between the *lai* and the romance, they were originally intended for the same kind of aristocratic audience. Such a twelfth-century audience we know had a passionate interest in the theory (and practice) of a refined kind of love such as Marie treats in the *Lais*. In some ways they would have seen their own world mirrored in Marie's fictional one: after all, they were of exalted rank, lived in castles, rode horses in forests, participated in tournaments and had love-affairs. Here again, the fairy-tale element may be visible if we are to regard the *Lais* at least partly as wish-fulfilment for a particular social class.

Also instructive is the relationship of the *lai* to the *fabliau*. *Fabliau* is the name given to a variety of short comic verse tale, in length and form comparable to the *lai*, whose period of composition coincides at least partly with that of the *lai*. Here is not the place for a full description of the *fabliau*, but suffice it to say that it could hardly be further removed from the *lai* in terms of spirit and content. Where the *lai* treats in a courtly style the lofty story of knights and ladies, the *fabliau* relates in often obscene language such subjects as the adulterous love of the merchant's wife and the parish priest, or gross practical jokes played by one character of dubious morals on another. Yet despite this fundamental distinction between the two genres, it is possible to argue that the *fabliau* is in some respects a parody of courtly literature and therefore by definition intended for the same audience.

Indeed, some poems which closely resemble *fabliaux* are actually called *lais* in the manuscripts (the title *Le Lai du Lecheor* will give an indication of the subject-matter), and this brings us on to the development of the *lai* after Marie de France. Of the anonymous *lais* written during Marie's period of activity, it may be said that most of them conform more or less to the pattern we have tried to sketch above, but one twelfth-century poem, *Le Lai du Cor*, describes a chastity-test of the ladies at Arthur's court. It is close to the *fabliau* by virtue of its subject-matter, and to the *lai* thanks to its Arthurian setting and the style in which it is written. These last features and its relative brevity may have led its author to call it a *lai* in the knowledge that it did not actually conform to the specific requirements of the genre. Such poems as this (*Lecheor* and *Ignauré* are others) may have been composed as parodies of the *lai* proper and may owe their denomination to the parodic intent. Other poems, such as Jean Renart's *Le Lai de l'Ombre* or the anonymous *Lai de l'Oiselet*, are clearly not meant as parodies of this kind and are yet still called *lais*. The simplest and most plausible explanation of this is that medieval literary terminology is at best rather flexible, and that whereas the word *lai* may have had the specific meaning of the Marie-type Breton *lai* in the twelfth century, its semantic field became enlarged in the thirteenth to cover other sorts of short courtly verse narrative. Recent genre criticism also suggests that, rather than seek to make strict definitions of genres, we may better view medieval vernacular literature as a system of interdependent types each with characteristic features. Some of these features, but not all, are interchangeable and may be found in works of a basically different kind. This is one way of looking at texts such as the *Lai du Lecheor*, or even Marie's *Equitan*, which has been said to resemble a *fabliau*.

Finally, a word should be said about the influence of the *Lais* outside French-language areas. It has been seen that in France other authors wrote *lais*, some in imitation of Marie. Abroad, the *Lais* seem to have enjoyed particular popularity in Scandinavia and England. An Old Norse translation of Marie's *Lais* and some anonymous ones was prepared towards the beginning of the thirteenth century by a certain Brother Robert for King Haakon I of Norway, the collection being generally referred to as the *Strengleikar*. The *Strengleikar* belong to a large body of Old Norse versions of Old French works produced during the same period for a monarch with a pronounced taste for French culture. While some of the adaptations of the longer French romances, such as those of Chrétien de Troyes, are reworked to a certain extent to cater for the tastes of a Scandinavian audience, the *Strengleikar* are quite faithful prose translations of the *Lais*. In England, a number of versions of *Lanval* have survived, the earliest dating from the middle of the fourteenth century, and a fragment of a version of *Le Fresne*. In addition, a number of original Middle English poems have been considered as *lais* and may have been written as a result of the popularity of the genre in French. The best known of these is Chaucer's *The Franklin's Tale*. The adaptations of *Lanval* form an interesting example of the different transformations an Old French poem can undergo at the hands of various poets with different intentions and different audiences in mind.

TRANSLATORS' NOTE

Until recently, the *Lais* of Marie de France could really be read in English only from Eugene Mason's translation, first published in 1911 and reprinted in 1954 and 1976. Mason's version is interesting as a piece of period prose, but is frequently little more than a paraphrase of passages he seems not to have properly understood. In 1978 there appeared a blank-verse translation by Joan Ferrante and Robert Hanning which, although infinitely superior to Mason's, lacks the kind of literal accuracy that, short of a poetic miracle, can alone convey the content of the original as precisely as possible.

Our aim has been to provide a plain English prose translation of Marie's *Lais* which renders them as closely as the semantic differences between Old French and Modern English will allow. We hope that both the general public and students of literature with no Old French will be able to read this translation with profit and pleasure (to use a medieval idea) in the knowledge that it is not too much a deformation of the original. Stylistically our final version differs in one major respect from our own earlier efforts and from Marie: we have renounced trying to reproduce Marie's rather short staccato phrases, often no more than a line long, and have given a little more 'flow' to the translation in order to make the *Lais* somewhat easier reading. We have, however, avoided adding to the sense, and have included 'ands', 'buts', etc., only where the context allowed. Those who know Modern French, or whose Old French is rusty, will be able to get an idea of the relationship between Marie's language and the modern idiom by looking at the texts of *Lanval*, *Laüstic* and *Chevrefoil* (in G. S. Burgess's edition) printed as an appendix.

We have not loaded our translation with explanatory or interpretative notes. With a few exceptions, anything that calls for comment is explained in the Index of Proper Names at the back. Moreover, many of the issues that are likely to be unfamiliar to the non-specialist are dealt with at some length in the Introduction. In cases of ambiguity in the Old French, we have simply opted for a particular meaning as being the most convincing in our view without commenting.

The *Lais* have been edited many times, but the standard editions are those of Karl Warnke (3rd edn, 1925), Alfred Ewert (1944 and reprints) and Jean Rychner (1966). As Ewert's edition of manuscript H is excellent and readily available in English-speaking countries, we have based our translation on it, although we have sometimes departed from his punctuation. To help the reader follow the poems in the Old French, line references to this edition have been provided at regular intervals.

Our translation of Marie's *Lais* appears in the wake of a revival of interest in the Middle Ages, as evidenced by the vast quantity of fantasy literature using medieval subject-matter or settings, and the phenomenal success of such novels as Umberto Eco's *The Name of the Rose*, as well as by general manifestations of medieval culture in library and museum exhibitions. We welcome this interest and hope that the present volume will help to dispense with the myth, still current in some circles, that medieval literature, pure and unadulterated, is inaccessible and irrelevant to the modern reader. As regards the *Lais* of Marie de France, nothing could be further from the truth.

We would like to thank Gill Gaughan and José Lanters for having read some of the *Lais* in various stages of completion. The late Mrs Betty Radice, former editor of the Penguin Classics series, made helpful comments and gave us much encouragement. For any remaining imperfections we are alone responsible.

Glyn S. Burgess, Liverpool
Keith Busby, Utrecht

The Lais of
Marie de France

PROLOGUE

Anyone who has received from God the gift of knowledge and true eloquence has a duty not to remain silent: rather should one be happy to reveal such talents. When a truly beneficial thing is heard by many people, it then enjoys its first blossom, but if it is widely praised its flowers are in full bloom. It was customary for the ancients, in the books which they wrote (Priscian testifies to this), to express themselves very obscurely so that those in later generations, who had to learn them, could provide a gloss for the text and put the finishing touches to their meaning. Men of learning were aware of this and their experience had taught them that the more time they spent studying texts the more subtle would be their understanding of them and they would be better able to avoid future mistakes. Anyone wishing to guard against vice should study intently and undertake a demanding task, whereby one can ward off and rid oneself of great suffering. For this reason I began to think of working on some good story and translating a Latin text into French, but this would scarcely have been worthwhile, for others have undertaken a similar task. So I thought of lays which I had heard and did not doubt, for I knew it full well, that they were composed, by those who first began them and put them into circulation, to perpetuate the memory of adventures they had heard. I myself have heard a number of them and do not wish to overlook or neglect them. I have put them into verse, made poems from them and worked on them late into the night.

In your honour, noble king, you who are so worthy and courtly, you to whom all joy pays homage and in whose heart all true virtue has taken root, did I set myself to assemble lays, to compose and to relate them in rhyme. In my heart, lord, I thought and decided that I should present them to you, so if it pleased you to accept them, you would bring me great happiness and I should rejoice evermore. Do not consider me presumptuous if I make so bold as to offer you this gift. Now hear the beginning.

1

GUIGEMAR

Whoever has good material for a story is grieved if the tale is not well told. Hear, my lords, the words of Marie, who, when she has the opportunity, does not squander her talents. Those who gain a good reputation should be commended, but when there exists in a country a man or woman of great renown, people who are envious of their abilities frequently speak insultingly of them in order to damage this reputation. Thus they start acting like a vicious, cowardly, treacherous dog which will bite others out of malice. But just because spiteful tittle-tattlers attempt to find fault with me I do not intend to give up. They have a right to make slanderous remarks.

I shall relate briefly to you stories which I know to be true and from which the Bretons have composed their lays. After these opening words I shall recount to you, just as it has been set down in writing, an adventure which happened in Brittany long ago. [1-26]

At that time Hoilas ruled the land, which was as often at war as at peace. The king had a baron who was lord of Liun. His name was Oridial and he enjoyed the confidence of his lord. He was a brave and valiant knight and his wife had borne him two children, a son and a beautiful daughter. The girl's name was Noguent and the boy was called Guigemar. There was no more handsome young man in the kingdom. His mother cherished him greatly and his father loved him dearly. As soon as he could bear to part with the boy, his father placed him in the service of another king. The young man was wise, brave and loved by everyone. When the time came that he had reached the right age and maturity of mind, the king dubbed him nobly and gave him whatever armour he desired. He left the court, dispensing lavish gifts before he departed, and went off to Flanders, where one could always find war and strife, in search of renown. At that time no one could find his equal as a knight, be it in Lorraine, Burgundy, Anjou or Gascony. [27–56] But Nature had done him such a grievous wrong that he never displayed the slightest interest in love. There was no lady or maiden on earth, however noble or beautiful, who would not have been happy to accept him as her lover, if he had sought her love. Women frequently made advances to him, but he was indifferent to them. He showed no visible interest in love and was thus considered a lost cause by stranger and friend alike.

At the height of his fame this noble knight returned to his homeland to see his father and his lord, his loving mother and his sister, who had all longed for his return. He had spent a month with them, I think, when the fancy took him to go hunting. That evening he summoned his knights, his hunters and his beaters, and in the morning went off into the forest, for hunting brought him great pleasure. They gathered in pursuit of a large stag and the hounds were unleashed. The hunters ran in front and the young man lingered behind. A servant carried his bow, his hunting-knife and his quiver. If the opportunity arose, he wished to be ready to shoot an arrow, before the animal had stirred. [57–88] In the heart of a large bush he saw a hind with its fawn; the beast was completely white with the antlers of a stag on its head. When the dog barked, it darted forth and Guigemar stretched his bow, fired his arrow and struck the animal in its forehead. Immediately the hind fell to the ground, but the arrow rebounded, hitting Guigemar in the thigh and going right through into the horse's flesh. He was forced to dismount and fell back on the thick grass beside the hind he had struck. The animal, wounded and in great pain, lamented in these words: 'Alas! I am mortally wounded. Vassal, you who have wounded me, let this be your fate. May you never find a cure, nor may any herb, root, doctor or potion ever heal the wound you have in your thigh until you are cured by a woman who will suffer for your love more pain and anguish than any other woman has ever known, and you will suffer likewise for her, so much so that all those who are in love, who have known love or are yet to experience it, will marvel at it. Be gone from here and leave me in peace.' [89–122]

Guigemar was seriously wounded and dismayed by what he had heard. He wondered where he could go to find a cure for his wound, for he did not intend to allow himself to die. He knew full well, and said to himself, that he had never seen any woman whom he could love or who could cure him of his suffering. He called to his squire: 'My friend, ride quickly and bring my companions back, for I should like to speak with them.' The young man rode off and Guigemar remained behind, lamenting his suffering. He bound his wound firmly and tightly with his shirt, then mounted his horse and departed. He was keen to get away, for he did not want any of his followers to come and hinder him, or attempt to detain him. A green path traversed the wood which led him out into an open space. There on the plain he saw a cliff and a mountain and from a stream which ran below a creek was formed. On it lay a harbour, in which there was a single ship whose sail Guigemar could see. The ship was fully prepared for departure, caulked inside and out in such a way that it was impossible to detect any joints. There was no peg or deck-rail which was not made of ebony. No gold on earth was worth more and the sail was made entirely of silk, very beautiful when unfurled. [123–60]

The knight was perturbed, as he had never heard say that ships could dock there. He rode forward, dismounted and in great pain climbed aboard expecting to find men in charge. But the ship was deserted and he saw no one. In the centre of the ship he discovered a bed whose posts and side-pieces were wrought after the fashion of Solomon, engraved with inlaid gold and made of cypress wood and white ivory. The quilt which lay upon it was of silk woven with gold. I could not set a price on the other bedclothes, but I can tell you this much about the pillow: no one who had lain his head on it would ever have white hair. The sable-skin coverlet was lined with Alexandrian silk, and on the prow of the ship stood two pure gold candelabra (even the less valuable of the two was worth a fortune) in which were lighted candles. [161–86] Guigemar marvelled at all this and in great pain from his wound reclined on the bed to rest. Then he rose intending to leave the ship, but he could not go back, as the ship was already on the high seas, speeding quickly away with him, the wind favourable and blowing gently. There was no question of his returning to land and he was grief-stricken, not knowing what to do. No wonder he was dismayed, for his wound was causing him great suffering. But he had to accept his fate and he prayed to God to take care of him, to bring him, if at all possible, to a safe harbour and protect him from death. He lay down on the bed and slept, but by now the worst was over and before evening he would reach the place where he would be cured, below an ancient city, capital of its realm. [187–208]

The lord who ruled over the city was a very old man whose wife was a lady of high birth. She was noble, courtly, beautiful and wise, and he was exceedingly jealous, as befitted his nature, for all old men are jealous and hate to be cuckolded. Such is the perversity of age. He did not take lightly the task of guarding her. In a garden at the foot of the keep was an enclosure, with a thick, high wall made of green marble. There was only a single point of entry, guarded day and night. The sea enclosed it on the other side, so it was impossible to get in or out, except by boat, should the need arise in the castle. As a secure place for his wife, the lord had constructed within the enclosure a chamber of incomparable beauty, at the entrance of which stood a chapel. [209–32] The walls of the chamber were covered in paintings in which Venus, the goddess of love, was skilfully depicted together with the nature and obligations of love; how it should be observed with loyalty and good service. In the painting Venus was shown as casting into a blazing fire the book in which Ovid teaches the art of controlling love and as excommunicating all those who read this book or adopted its teachings. In this room the lady was imprisoned. To serve her the lord had provided her with a noble and intelligent maiden, who was his niece, his sister's daughter. The two loved each other dearly, and when the husband was away, the girl remained with her until his return. No one, man or woman, could have gained access to this spot, or escaped from this walled enclosure. An old priest with hoary-white hair guarded the key to the gate; he had lost his lower members, otherwise he would not have been trusted. He recited the divine service and served her at table. [233–60]

That very day, in the early afternoon, the lady had made her way into the garden. She had fallen asleep after her meal, and then gone with her maiden in search of recreation. They looked down towards the shore and saw the ship rising on the waves as it sailed into the harbour, but they could not see how it was being steered. The lady wanted to turn and run: no wonder she was afraid. Her face became quite flushed. But the maiden, who was wise and of bolder disposition, comforted and reassured her. They hastened towards the ship, and taking off her coat, the girl boarded the beautiful vessel. She found there no living thing apart from the sleeping knight. Seeing how pale he was the girl assumed he was dead. She stopped and looked at him, then returned, called hastily to her lady and gave her a true account. She lamented the dead man she had seen and the lady replied: 'Let us go together, and, if he is dead, we shall bury him. Our priest will help us. But if I find him alive, he will speak to us.' They made their way without delay, the lady leading and the maiden following. [261–92] When she entered the ship, the lady paused before the bed; she looked at the knight and grieved deeply over his handsome body, which filled her with sorrow. She deplored the loss of this young life. Placing her hand on his chest, she discovered that it was warm and his heart sound, beating beneath his ribs. The knight who was sleeping awoke and saw her. Joyfully he greeted her, knowing full well that he had reached the shore. The lady, tearful and perturbed, responded to him politely and inquired how he came to be there, from what land he was, and whether he had been exiled through war. 'My lady,' he said, 'that is not the case. But if you wish me to tell you the truth, I shall do so and withhold nothing from you. I have come from Brittany and today I went hunting in a wood, where I shot a white hind. The arrow rebounded, giving me such a wound in the thigh that I think a cure is impossible. The hind lamented and spoke to me, cursing me and swearing that my only cure would be at the hands of a damsel. I do not know where she is to be found. But when I heard my fate I hurriedly left the wood, saw this ship in a harbour and foolishly got on board. The ship quickly sailed away with me in it. I do not know where I am or what this city is called. Fair lady, I beg you in God's name, please help me, for I do not know where to go, or how to steer the ship.' [293–336] She replied: 'My dear lord, I shall gladly help you: this city belongs to my husband, as does all the surrounding country. He is a rich man of high lineage, but he is very old and fearfully jealous. On my honour, he has imprisoned me in this enclosure. There is only a single entrance and an old priest guards the gate: may God grant that he be consumed by hell-fire! I am shut in here day and night, and not once would I dare leave without his permission or unless my lord asked for me. My bedchamber and my chapel are here and this maiden is with me. If you wish to remain until you can travel more easily, we shall be pleased to shelter you and will serve you wholeheartedly.' When he heard these words, Guigemar thanked the lady politely and said he would stay with her. He raised himself up off the bed and they supported him with some difficulty. The lady took the young man to her chamber, where he was placed on the maiden's bed, behind a canopy which served as a curtain in the bedroom. [337–68] They brought water in golden basins, washed his wounded thigh, then removed the surrounding blood with a fine piece of white linen and bound it tightly. They treated him with loving care, and when their evening meal arrived the maiden retained sufficient for the knight's needs, so that he was well supplied with food and drink. But love had now pierced him to the quick and his heart was greatly disturbed. For the lady had wounded him so deeply that he had completely forgotten his homeland. He felt no pain from the wound in his thigh, yet he sighed in great anguish and asked the maiden serving him to let him sleep. As he had dismissed her, she returned to her mistress, who was, like Guigemar, affected by the ardour which had kindled within her heart. [369–92]

The knight remained alone, mournful and downcast. He did not yet realize the cause, but at least he knew that, if he were not cured by the lady, his death would be assured. 'Alas,' he said, 'what shall I do? I shall go and ask her to have mercy and pity on this forlorn wretch. If she refuses my request and is arrogant or harsh, then I must die of grief and languish forever from this ill.' Then he sighed, but soon a new thought struck him: he told himself that suffering was inevitable, for there was no alternative. He spent a sleepless night, sighing in anguish. In his mind he constantly recalled her speech, her appearance, her sparkling eyes and beautiful mouth: the pain she caused reached deep into his heart. In a whisper he begged her for mercy and almost called her his beloved. If he had only known her feelings and how love was afflicting her, he would, I think, have been happy. A little comfort would have gone some way towards assuaging the suffering which had drained his face of colour. But if he was feeling anguish for love of her, the lady had no reason to feel superior. Next morning, before daybreak, she rose, bewailing the fact that she had spent the night awake. Love, which was torturing her, was the cause.

The maiden, who was with her, could see from her appearance that she was in love with the knight who was lodging in her chamber for his cure. But the lady did not know whether or not he loved her. When she entered the chapel, the maiden went to the knight. [393–438]

She sat down by the bed and he addressed her in these words: 'My friend, where has my lady gone? Why did she rise so early?' Then he fell silent and sighed. The maiden replied: 'My lord, you are in love: mind you do not conceal the fact too long. Your love may well have found a true home. The man who wishes to love my lady must keep her constantly in his thoughts and, if you remain faithful to each other, the love between you will be right and proper. You are handsome and she is beautiful.' He replied to the damsel: 'I am inflamed with such love that, if I do not receive succour, I shall be in a sorry plight. Help me, my sweet friend. What shall I do with this love?' The maiden comforted him most tenderly, and assured him of her assistance and good offices, wherever possible: she was most courtly and noble. [439–64]

When the lady had heard mass, she returned, aware of her obligations. She wished to know what the knight was doing, if he was awake or asleep. The love for him which had entered her heart had not abated. The maiden summoned her to approach the knight. She would have ample time to explain her feelings to him, no matter what the consequences. He greeted her and she him. They were both suffering great distress, but he did not dare ask anything of her, as he was a stranger from a foreign land. He was afraid that, if he spoke to her of his emotions, she would hate him and send him away. But he who does not let his infirmity be known can scarcely expect to receive a cure. Love is an invisible wound within the body, and, since it has its source in nature, it is a long-lasting ill. For many it is the butt of jokes, as for those ignoble courtiers who philander around the world and then boast of their deeds. That is not love, but rather foolishness, wickedness and debauchery. A loyal partner, once discovered, should be served, loved and obeyed. [465–95]

Guigemar was very much in love and either had to receive relief or be forced to live a life of misery. Love emboldened him to reveal his feelings to her. 'My lady,' he said, 'I am dying because of you; my heart is giving me great pain. If you are not willing to cure me, then it must all end in my death. I am asking for your love. Fair one, do not refuse me.' When she heard his words, she replied fittingly, and said lightly: 'Friend, such a decision would be over-hasty: I am not accustomed to such requests.' 'My lady,' he replied, 'in God's name, have mercy on me! Do not be distressed if I say this: a woman who is always fickle likes to extend courtship in order to enhance her own esteem and so that the man will not realize that she has experienced the pleasure of love. But the well-intentioned lady, who is worthy and wise, should not be too harsh towards a man, if she finds him to her liking; she should rather love him and enjoy his love. Before anyone discovers or hears of their love, they will greatly profit from it. Fair lady, let us put an end to this discussion.' The lady recognized the truth of his words and granted him her love without delay. He kissed her and henceforth was at peace. They lay together and talked, kissing and embracing. May the final act, which others are accustomed to enjoy, give them pleasure. [496–534]

Guigemar was with her for a year and a half, I believe, and their life gave them great delight. But fortune, never unmindful of her duties, can soon turn her wheel. One man takes a fall, another rises; so it was in their case, for they were soon discovered.

One summer morning the lady lay next to the young man. She kissed his mouth and his face, then said: 'My fair, sweet friend, my heart tells me I am about to lose you: we are going to be discovered. If you die, I too wish to die; and if you manage to escape, you will find another love and I shall remain here, grief-stricken.' 'My lady,' he replied, 'do not say such things! May I have no peace or joy, if I ever turn to another woman. Do not be afraid.' 'Beloved, give me assurance of this. Hand me your shirt and I shall tie a knot in the tailpiece. I give you leave, wherever you may be, to love the woman who can undo the knot and untie it.' He gave it to her, made his pledge and she tied the knot in such a way that no woman could undo it, without the help of scissors or a knife. She gave him back the shirt and he took it on the understanding that she would make a similar pledge to him, by means of a belt which she would gird about her bare flesh and draw tightly around her loins. He encouraged her to love any man who could open the buckle without tearing or severing it. Then he kissed her and let the matter drop. [535–76]

That day they were perceived, discovered, found and seen by a cunning chamberlain sent by her husband. He wished to speak to the lady, but could not gain access to the chamber. Seeing them through a window, he reported the matter to his lord. When the lord heard him, it gave him more pain than he had ever known. Summoning three trustworthy men, he went forthwith to the chamber, had the door broken down and discovered the knight, whereupon in great anger he ordered him to be killed. Guigemar stood up, quite unafraid. He seized a large fir-wood pole, used for hanging clothes, and waited for them, intending to make someone suffer: before any of his adversaries had got near him, he would have maimed them one and all. The lord looked at him intently, asked who he was, where he was from and how he had entered. Guigemar explained how he had arrived, how the lady had retained him, and all about the prophecy of the wounded hind, about the ship and his wound. Now he was entirely in the lord's power. The lord replied that he did not believe him, but that if things were as he stated and he could find the ship, he would then put him out to sea. If he survived, he would be sorry, and if he drowned, he would be delighted. When the lord had given this assurance, they went together to the harbour, where they found the ship and put him aboard. [577–619] The ship set sail, taking him back to his own country, and got under way without delay while the knight sighed and wept, lamenting the lady frequently and praying to Almighty God to let him die a quick death without ever reaching land, if he could not see again his beloved whom he desired more than his life. His grief was unabated until the ship arrived in the harbour where it had first been discovered, very close to his homeland. Guigemar disembarked as quickly as possible and recognized a young man whom he had raised and who was leading a charger for a knight he was following. Guigemar called to the youth, who looked round, saw his lord and dismounted. He offered him the horse, and they rode off together. All his friends were full of joy that he had been found. But although Guigemar was highly regarded in his land, he was constantly sad and downcast. They wanted him to take a wife, but he would not hear of the idea. Never would he take a wife, for love or money, unless she could undo his shirt without tearing it. The news travelled throughout Brittany and there was no lady or maiden who did not make the attempt, but they were never successful. [620–54]

I must to tell you about the lady whom Guigemar loved so much. On the advice of one of his barons her husband imprisoned her in a tower of dark-hued marble. She suffered during the day and at night it was worse. No man on earth could describe the great pain, agony, anguish and grief which the lady experienced in the tower, where she spent, I think, over two years. She knew no joy or pleasure and frequently mourned for her beloved: 'Guigemar, lord, how sad that I met you! I prefer to die a speedy death rather than suffer this misfortune too long. Beloved, if I could escape, I should drown myself just where you were put to sea!' Then she rose: distraught, she went to the door and found no key or bolt. Thus she had the chance to escape, and no one at all hindered her. She went to the harbour where she found the ship. It was attached to the rock where she intended to drown herself. Seeing it, she went aboard. But she had only one thing on her mind: it was there that her beloved must have drowned. Suddenly she could not remain upright. If she could have reached the side, she would have thrown herself overboard, so great was the anguish she was suffering. The ship set sail, carrying her quickly away, and reached port in Brittany, beneath a fine, strong castle. [655–90] The lord of the castle, whose name was Meriaduc, was waging war against a neighbour, and for that purpose he had risen early, intending to send his men forth to inflict losses on his enemy. Standing at a window, he saw the ship arrive. He went down some steps and summoned a chamberlain; they went quickly towards the ship, climbed the ladder and boarded it; there they found the lady who was as lovely as a fairy. Taking her by the mantle, the lord took her off to his castle, delighted by his discovery, as the lady was extremely beautiful. He knew full well that, whatever the reason for her being on the ship, she was of a noble lineage, and he conceived a love for her greater than for any other woman. He had a very beautiful, young sister in his chamber, to whom he entrusted the lady. She was well served and honoured, richly dressed and attired, but she was always sad and downcast. The lord often went to speak to her, for he loved her with all his heart. He begged her for her love, but she remained indifferent to his pleas. Instead she showed him the belt: she would love only the man who could undo the knot without tearing it. When he heard her, he replied angrily: 'There is also in this land a knight of very great renown who refuses in similar fashion to take a wife because of a shirt with its right flap knotted. It cannot be untied, except by using scissors or a knife. I think it was you who tied that knot.' When she heard this, she sighed and almost fainted. He took her in his arms, cut the lacing of her tunic, and endeavoured to open the belt, but to no avail. Afterwards all the knights in the land were summoned to make the attempt. [691–742]

Thus things remained for a long while until the occasion of a tournament which Meriaduc proclaimed against his enemy. He summoned knights and retained them, confident that Guigemar would come. He asked for Guigemar's presence as a friend and companion, promising him recompense and beseeching him not to fail him in his hour of need, but to come to his assistance. Guigemar arrived, richly attired, bringing with him more than a hundred knights. Meriaduc lodged him in his tower with great honour, then called for his sister to greet him, sending two knights with orders that she should adorn herself and come forward, bringing the lady whom he loved so much. She obeyed his commands, and richly attired, the two entered the hall hand in hand. The lady was sad and pale, and hearing Guigemar's name she lost her balance. If the sister had not held her, she would have fallen to the ground. The knight rose to greet them; he saw the lady and looked at her appearance and bearing. Stepping back a pace, he said: 'Is this my sweet friend, my hope, my heart, my life, my beautiful lady who loved me? Where has she come from? Who brought her here? But I have been indulging in very foolish thoughts. I know it is not she; women look very much alike. My mind has been disturbed for nothing, but since she resembles the woman for whom my heart sighs and trembles I shall gladly speak to her.' [743–83] Then the knight went forward, kissed her and sat her down beside him; he spoke no other word than his request for her to be seated. Meriaduc looked at them, very unhappy at the way things appeared. He called laughingly to Guigemar: 'Lord, if you wish, this maiden will see if she can manage to undo your shirt.' Guigemar replied: 'I accept,' and he summoned a chamberlain who looked after the shirt, ordering it to be brought to him. It was given to the maiden, but she did not untie it. She recognized the knot easily, but her heart was too full of anguish; she would have been willing to try, if she could and if she dared. Meriaduc realized this and it grieved him. All he could do was to say: 'Lady, try to undo it.' When she heard the command, she took the flap of the shirt and, to the knight's astonishment, untied it easily. He recognized her, but nevertheless he was not completely convinced. He addressed her in these words: 'Beloved, sweet creature, tell me the truth: let me see your body and the belt with which I girded you.' He placed his hands on her hips and found the belt. [784–821] 'Beloved,' he said, 'how fortunate that I have discovered you like this! Who brought you here?' She related to him the grief, the great suffering and the dreariness of the prison in which she had been, and how things had turned out, how she escaped with the intention of drowning herself, but had found the ship, gone on board and arrived at this port; and how the knight had retained her and looked after her with great honour, but had constantly made advances to her. Now she was once more full of joy: 'Beloved, take your sweetheart away!' Guigemar rose. 'My lords,' he said, 'listen to me! I have discovered a friend whom I thought I had lost forever. I implore Meriaduc in his mercy to restore her to me. I shall become his vassal and serve him for two or three years with a hundred knights or more.' Then Meriaduc replied: 'Guigemar, I am not in sufficiently dire straits or so troubled by war that you should request this of me. I found her and I shall keep her and defend her against you.' [822–52]

When Guigemar heard this, he quickly commanded his men to mount. He departed, issuing a challenge to Meriaduc. It grieved him very much to leave his beloved. He took with him every knight in the town who had come for the tournament. Each one pledged his support: they would accompany him wherever he went: the man who failed him now would be disgraced. That night they arrived at the castle of Meriaduc's opponent. The lord lodged them and was happy to have Guigemar and his assistance. He realized the war was over. Next day they rose early and everyone in the lodgings equipped himself, whereupon they made a noisy exit from the town with Guigemar out in front. They reached the castle and attacked it, but it was strong and they could not take it. Guigemar besieged the town and would not leave until it was captured. His friends and followers increased in number so much that he starved all those inside. He captured and destroyed the castle and killed the lord within.

With great joy he took away his beloved. Now his tribulations were over. [853–82]

The lay of *Guigemar*, which is performed on harp and rote,[1] was composed from the tale you have heard. The melody is pleasing to the ear. [883–6]

II

EQUITAN

The Bretons, who lived in Brittany, were fine and noble people. In days gone by these valiant, courtly and noble men composed lays for posterity and thus preserved them from oblivion. These lays were based on adventures they had heard and which had befallen many a person. One of them, which I have heard recited, should not be forgotten. It concerns Equitan, a most courtly man, lord of Nantes, justiciary and king. [1-12]

Equitan enjoyed a fine reputation and was greatly loved in his land. He adored pleasure and amorous dalliance: for this reason he upheld the principles of chivalry. Those who lack a full comprehension and understanding of love show no thought for their lives. Such is the nature of love that no one under its sway can retain command over reason. Equitan had a seneschal, a good knight, brave and loyal, who took care of his entire territory, governing it and administering its justice. Never, except in time of war, would the king have forsaken his hunting, his pleasures or his river sports, whatever the need might have been. [13-28]

As his wedded wife the seneschal had a woman who was to bring great misfortune to the land. She was a lady of fine breeding and extremely beautiful with a noble body and good bearing. Nature had spared no pains when fashioning her: her eyes sparkled, her face and mouth were beautiful and her nose was well set. She had no equal in the kingdom, and the king, having often heard her praised, frequently sent her greetings and gifts. They had never met, but he conceived a desire for her and seized the first opportunity to speak with her. He went hunting in her region on his own and on returning from his sport took lodging for the night in the place where the seneschal dwelt, in the very castle where the lady was to be found. He had ample occasion to speak with her, to express his feelings and display his fine qualities. He found her most courtly and wise, beautiful in body and countenance, of fair appearance and cheerful disposition. [29–53]

Love admitted him into her service and let fly in his direction an arrow which left a very deep wound in him. It was launched at his heart and there it became firmly fixed. Wisdom and understanding were of no avail. Through the lady Love caught him unawares, with the result that he was distraught and overcome with sadness. Unable to withstand its power, he was forced to give Love his full attention. That night he neither slept nor rested, but spent his time reproaching and reprimanding himself. 'Alas,' he said, 'what destiny brought me to this region? Because of this lady I have seen, my heart has been overwhelmed by a pain so great that my whole body trembles. I think I have no option but to love her. Yet, if I did love her, I should be acting wrongly, as she is the seneschal's wife. I ought to keep faith with him and love him, just as I want him to do with me. If he managed somehow to find out about the love, I know full well it would grieve him. But nevertheless, it would be far worse if I were to be laid low because of her. How sad if such a beautiful woman were not in love or had no lover! How could she be a true courtly lady, if she had no true love? There is no man on earth who would not benefit greatly, if she loved him. If the seneschal were to hear tell of it, he should not distress himself too much; he cannot keep her entirely for himself. I am certainly willing to share her with him.' [54–88] Having spoken thus, he uttered a sigh, then lay in bed, deep in thought. Later he spoke, saying: 'Why am I so distressed and alarmed? I do not yet know, indeed I have never known, if she would be willing to take me as her lover. But I shall soon find out. If she felt as I do, this agony of mine would disappear. Oh God! Daybreak is so long in coming. I can get no rest. Many hours have elapsed since I came to bed last night.' [89–100]

The king stayed awake until morning, which he awaited with impatience. Then he rose and set off on his hunt. But he soon turned back, saying how very ill he was, and returned to his chamber to lie down. The seneschal was grieved by this, not realizing the cause of the illness or why the king was feverish. His wife was the true reason for it. To please and comfort him the king had her come and speak with him, whereupon he disclosed his feelings to her, letting her know that he was dying because of her and that she was well able to bring comfort to him or to cause his death. 'My lord,' said the lady, 'I must have time to reflect on this. At this stage I am not sure what to do. You are a king of great nobility; I am not wealthy enough to be the object of your love or passion. If you had your way with me, I know well and am in no doubt that you would soon abandon me and I should be very much worse off. If it should come about that I loved you and granted your request, our love would not be shared equally. Because you are a powerful king and my husband is your vassal, you would expect, as I see it, to be the lord and master in love as well. [101–36] Love is not honourable, unless it is based on equality. A poor man, if he is loyal and possesses wisdom and merit, is of greater worth and his love more joyful than that of a prince or king who lacks loyalty. If anyone places his love higher than is appropriate for his own station in life, he must fear all manner of things. The powerful man is convinced that no one can steal away his beloved over whom he intends to exercise his seigneurial right.' To this Equitan replied: 'My lady, I beg you. Do not say such things! Such men are not truly courtly. This is the sort of deal struck between merchants who, to acquire wealth or a large fief, expend much effort for some unseemly purpose. Any wise and courtly lady of noble disposition, who sets a high price on her love and is not fickle, deserves to be sought after by a rich prince in his castle, and loved well and loyally, even if her only possession is her mantle. Those who are fickle in love and resort to trickery end up becoming a laughing-stock and are deceived in their turn. We have seen many cases of this. It is no surprise that a man should lose out, if his actions warrant it. My dearest lady, I surrender myself to you! Do not regard me as your king, but as your vassal and lover. I swear to you in all honesty that I shall do your bidding. Do not let me die because of you. You can be the mistress and I the servant; you the haughty one and I the suppliant.' So long did the king speak with her and so ardently did he beg for mercy that she promised him her love and gave him her body. By an exchange of rings they took possession of each other and pledged their faith. They kept this faith well and loved each other dearly. It was later to be the cause of their death. [137–84]

Their love lasted a long time and remained undetected. When they had arranged to meet and speak with each other, the king told his followers he was to be bled in private. The doors of the bedchamber were closed. Never would anyone have dared to enter without the king's summons. The seneschal presided over the court, hearing the pleas and accusations. The king loved the lady for a long time and had no desire for any other woman. He did not wish to marry and refused to permit the subject to be discussed. The courtiers thought ill of him for this, to the point where the matter often came to the ears of the seneschal's wife. It distressed her greatly and she feared losing him. So next time she was able to talk to him, when she ought to have been full of joy, kissing him, holding him in tight embrace and enjoying herself with him, she wept bitterly and was plunged into grief. The king asked her how this could be. [185-211] The lady replied: 'Lord, I am weeping for our love which brings great sorrow to me. You will take a wife, a king's daughter, and leave me. I have heard this mentioned often and I am sure it will happen. What would become of me, unhappy wretch? Through you my death is inevitable. For I know of no other consolation.' The king replied with great tenderness: 'My fair one, do not be afraid. I shall certainly never take a wife or leave you for another. Accept this as the truth and believe me: if your husband were dead, I should make you my queen and my lady. I should not be deterred from this for anyone's sake.' The lady thanked him and expressed her gratitude. If he promised not to abandon her for another woman, she would, she said, soon bring about her husband's death. It would be easy to arrange, provided he were willing to help her. [212-36] He agreed that he would do so. Regardless of the consequences he would do his utmost to accomplish whatever she commanded. 'Lord,' she said, 'please come hunting in the forest in the region where I live. Stay in my husband's castle, be bled there and take a bath on the third day. My husband will be bled and take a bath with you. Make sure you tell him to keep you company. I shall have the baths heated and the two tubs brought in. The water in his bath will be so boiling hot that no mortal man could escape scalding or destruction, before he has settled down in it. When he has been scalded to death, summon your vassals and his. Show them how he suddenly died in the bath.' The king promised faithfully to do what she wished. [237-62]

Less than three months later the king went hunting in the region.

He had himself bled together with his seneschal, as a precaution against illness. On the third day he declared that he would take a bath. The seneschal assented to this and the king said: 'You will bathe with me.' The seneschal replied: 'I agree.' The lady had the baths heated and the two tubs brought in. As planned, each of the tubs was placed in front of the bed. She had the boiling water brought in for the seneschal, who had gone out in search of relaxation. The lady came to speak to the king and he made her sit down beside him. They lay down on the lord's bed and took their pleasure. They lay there together. Because of the tub which stood before them they had the door guarded by a maiden who was to stand there. [263–82] Suddenly the seneschal returned and banged on the door which the girl kept closed. He gave it such a violent blow that it was forced open, whereupon he discovered the king and his wife in each other's arms. The king looked up and saw him approaching. To conceal his wickedness he jumped feet first into the tub, completely naked. He paid no heed to the danger involved and was scalded to death. His evil plan had rebounded on him, whereas the seneschal was safe and sound. He saw just what had happened to the king. Seizing his wife immediately, he tossed her head first into the bath. Thus they died together, the king first, then the woman with him. Anyone willing to listen to reason could profit from this cautionary tale. Evil can easily rebound on him who seeks another's misfortune. [283–310]

All this happened as I have described. The Bretons composed a lay on this subject, about how Equitan died and about the lady who loved him so dearly. [311–14]

III

LE FRESNE

I shall tell you the lay of *Le Fresne* according to the story which I know. [1–2]

There once lived in Brittany two knights who were neighbours, rich and wealthy men, worthy and valiant knights from the same region. They had both taken a wife and one of the ladies conceived, giving birth to two children when her time came. Her husband was happy and joyful, and because of his joy sent word to his neighbour that his family was increased, as his wife had had two sons. He also said that he would present one of them to him so that he could stand godfather to the boy who would be named after him. The rich man was seated at table when the messenger arrived and knelt before the high table. He delivered his message fully, whereupon the lord gave thanks to God and offered him a fine horse. This knight's wife, who was sitting next to him at table, smiled, for she was deceitful and arrogant, prone to slander and envy. [3–28] She spoke foolishly and said in front of the whole household: 'So help me God, I am astonished that this worthy man decided to inform my husband of his shame and dishonour, that his wife has had two sons. They have both incurred shame because of it, for we know what is at issue here: it has never occurred that a woman gave birth to two sons at once, nor ever will, unless two men are the cause of it.' Her husband stared at her and reproached her severely. 'Lady,' he said, 'no more! You should not speak thus! The truth is that this lady has been of good repute.' Those in the house took note of these words which were repeated and became widely known throughout all Brittany: the lady was much hated and later suffered because of them, for all women who heard these words, both poor and rich, hated her as a result. The bearer of the message told his lord everything and when he heard the account he was saddened and did not know what to do. For this reason he hated the worthy woman and was highly mistrustful of her, keeping her in close custody without her having deserved it. [29–64]

The same year the slanderer herself conceived twins and now her neighbour was avenged. She carried them until her time came and then had two daughters, which grieved and distressed her greatly. She lamented to herself: 'Alas!' she said, 'what shall I do? Now I shall never have esteem or honour! I am shamed, in truth, for neither my husband nor all his family will ever believe me, to be sure, when they hear of this adventure. I have been my own judge: I spoke ill of all women. Did I not say that it has never been the case and we had never seen it happen that a woman has had two children unless she has known two men? Now I have twins and it seems that I am paying the price. Whoever slanders and lies about others does not know what retribution awaits him. One can speak ill of someone who is more praiseworthy than oneself. To ward off shame, I shall have to murder one of the children: I would rather make amends with God than shame and dishonour myself.' Those who were in the chamber comforted her and said that they would not allow it, for killing was not a trifle. [65–98]

The lady had a maid of very noble birth who had long taken care of her and brought her up, loved her and cherished her greatly. The girl heard her lady crying, lamenting grievously and moaning, and this caused her great anguish. She came and comforted her: 'Lady,' she said, 'it is no use. You will do well to abandon this sadness! Let me have one of the children and I shall rid you of her so that you will never be shamed or see her ever again. I shall abandon her in a church to which I shall carry her safe and sound. Some worthy man will find her and, if it please God, raise her.' The lady heard what she said and was overjoyed, promising her that she would receive a good reward if she performed this service. They wrapped the noble child in a cloth of fine linen and then placed over her the finest piece of striped brocade which her husband had brought from Constantinople, where he had been. With a piece of her ribbon, the lady attached to the child's arm a large ring made from an ounce of pure gold, with a ruby set in it and lettering on the band. Wherever she was found, people would then truly know that she was of noble birth. The damsel took the child and left the chamber forthwith. [99–136] That night, when all was dark, she left the town and took to a wide path which led her into the forest, and making her way through the wood by keeping to the main path, she emerged on the other side with the child. Far away to the right she had heard dogs barking and cocks crowing, and there she knew she could find a town. The damsel went quickly in the direction of the barking and entered a rich and fair town where there was an exceptionally wealthy and well-endowed abbey. I think it housed nuns with an abbess to watch over them. The girl saw the church, the towers, the walls and the bell-tower, and approached hurriedly, stopping before the door. She put down the child she was carrying, knelt humbly and began her prayer: 'God,' she said, 'by your holy name, if it please you, Lord, keep this infant from perishing.' When she had finished her prayer, she looked behind her and saw a wide ash-tree, luxuriant and with many boughs. It branched out into four forks and had been planted there as a source of shade. She took the child in her arms, ran up to the ash-tree, placed the child in it and then left her, commending her to the one true God. The damsel returned and told her lady what she had done. [137–76]

There was a porter at the abbey who opened the outer door of the church by which people entered to hear the service. That night he arose early, lit candles and lamps, rang the bells and opened the door. When he saw the garments on the ash-tree his only thought was that someone had stolen them and put them there. He made his way over to the tree as soon as he could, felt with his hand and thus found the child. He then gave thanks to God, took the child and returned home, not wanting to leave it there. He had a widowed daughter who had in the cradle a baby she was suckling. The worthy man called out: 'Daughter, arise, arise! Light a fire and candles! I have brought here a child which I found outside in the ash-tree. Suckle it with your milk for me, keep it warm, and bathe it!' [177–202] She obeyed him and lit the fire, taking the child and making it warm. She bathed it well and then suckled it with her milk. On its arm she found the ring, and when they saw the rich and beautiful cloth of silk, they were sure that she was born of high degree. That day after the service, when the abbess left the church, the porter went to talk to her, for he wanted to tell her the story of how he had found the child. The abbess commanded it to be brought before her just as it had been found and so the porter went to his house and willingly brought the child to show her. She looked at the girl intently and said she would have her brought up as her niece, forbidding the porter to say anything about it. She herself raised the child and because she had been found in the ash-tree, they named her Le Fresne, which was what people then called her. [203–30]

The lady kept her secretly for a while as her niece and the girl was raised within the bounds of the abbey. When she reached the age when Nature forms beauty, there was no fairer, no more courtly girl in Brittany, for she was noble and cultivated, both in appearance and in speech. No one who had seen her would have failed to love and admire her greatly.

In Dol there lived the best lord there has ever been. I shall now tell you his name: in his country they called him Gurun, and he had heard tell of the maiden and began to love her. He went to a tournament and returned by way of the abbey, asking to see the girl. The abbess showed her to him, and when he saw that she was very beautiful and well educated, wise, courtly and well brought-up, he said to himself that he would henceforth consider himself unfortunate if he did not have her love. He was distraught and did not know what to do, for if he were to return too often the abbess would notice and he would never see the girl again. He thought of a solution: he would increase the wealth of the abbey and give it a great deal of his land, thereby enriching it for all time, for he wanted to have a lord's rights to a dwelling-place and residence. In order to join their community he gave them a generous portion of his wealth, but his motive was other than remission for his sins. He went there often to talk to the girl, and begged her and promised her so much that she granted what he sought. [231–74]

When he was sure of her love, he spoke to her one day: 'Fair one, you have now made me your love. Come away with me for good! I assure you that should your aunt notice she would be most aggrieved and extremely angry if you became pregnant in her house. If you accept my advice, you will come away with me. Be sure I shall never fail you and shall provide for you well.' As she loved him deeply, she granted him his request and went away with him: he took her to his castle. She took her brocade and ring, for that might yet turn out to her advantage. The abbess had given them to her and told her what had happened when first she had been sent to her and placed in the ash-tree. Whoever had sent her in the first place had given her the brocade and the ring, but no other riches accompanied her; she had then raised her as her niece. The girl kept the brocade and ring and put them in a casket which she carried with her, for she did not want to leave or forget it. The knight who took her away cherished and loved her greatly, as did all his men and his servants. There was not one, humble or great, who did not love and honour her for her nobility. [275–312]

After she had been with Gurun for some time, the landed knights reproached him for it severely, and they often spoke to him saying that he should take a noble wife and free himself from Le Fresne. They would be happier if he had an heir to inherit his land and it would be a grievous loss if he did not have a child by a wife on account of his concubine. They would never more consider him their lord, nor serve him willingly, if he did not do their bidding. The knight agreed to take a wife on their advice and so they looked to see where one might be found. 'Lord,' they said, 'close to us here is a worthy man quite your equal who has a daughter as his heir: much land will come with her. The damsel is called La Codre and in all the land there is none so fair. In exchange for Le Fresne, whom you will give up, you will have La Codre. On the hazel there are nuts to be enjoyed, but the ash never bears fruit. We shall seek to obtain the damsel, and if it please God, we shall give her to you.' Thus they sought this marriage and assent was given by all parties. Alas! what a misfortune that the worthy men did not know the story of these damsels who were twin sisters! Le Fresne was kept hidden from the other girl, who was then married to Le Fresne's beloved. When she learned of the marriage, Le Fresne showed no displeasure but served her lord properly and honoured all his people. The knights of his household, the squires and the serving-boys, grieved much because they were going to lose her. [313–58]

On the day set for their marriage Gurun summoned his friends, and his vassal the Archbishop of Dol was there. They brought Gurun's wife to him, but her mother, who accompanied her, was afraid of the girl whom he loved so much, lest she try to cause ill-will between her daughter and her husband. She planned to cast her out of her own house and advise her son-in-law to marry her to a worthy man, for in this way she could be rid of her.

The wedding was richly celebrated and there was much merrymaking. The damsel was in the bedchamber but gave no sign that anything she had seen had upset her, not even sufficiently to anger her. She served the lady willingly and properly so that those who saw her, both men and women, marvelled at it. Her mother looked at her intently, and esteemed and loved her in her heart. She thought and said to herself that if she had known the kind of person Le Fresne was, she would not have suffered harm because of her daughter La Codre, nor would her lord have been taken from her. [359–88]

That night, when the bed in which the wife was to lie was being prepared, the damsel went there and took off her cloak. She summoned the chamberlains and showed them how her lord wanted the bed made, for she had often seen it done. When they had made the bed ready, they covered it with a sheet made from old dress-material. The damsel saw it and was dissatisfied, for it did not seem right to her. She opened a chest, took out her brocade and, to honour him, put it on her lord's bed. The Archbishop was there to bless them and make the sign of the cross over them, for this was part of his duty. When the chamber was empty, the lady brought her daughter, whom she wanted to get ready for bed, and told her to undress. She saw the brocade on the bed, the like of which she had never seen, save for the one she had given away with the daughter she had concealed. Then she remembered her and trembled in her heart. She called the chamberlain to her. [389–419] 'Tell me,' she said, 'on your faith, where was this fine brocade found?' 'Lady,' he said, 'I shall tell you: the damsel brought it and cast it over this coverlet which she did not like. I think that the brocade is hers.' The lady called her and she came. When she had taken off her cloak, her mother spoke to her: 'Fair friend, do not conceal it from me. Where was this good brocade found? How did you acquire it? Who gave it to you? Tell me from whom you received it!' The girl answered her: 'Lady, my aunt, the abbess, who raised me, gave it to me and ordered me to keep it. Those who sent me to be brought up gave me that and a ring.' 'Fair one, may I see the ring?' 'Yes, my lady, with pleasure.' She brought her the ring and the lady looked at it carefully, easily recognizing it and the brocade. She had no doubt, for she now knew for sure that this was indeed her daughter, and, for all to hear, she said openly: 'You are my daughter, fair friend!' [420–50] Because of the emotion she felt she fell back and fainted. When she arose from her swoon, she sent for her husband straightaway and he came, quite frightened. When he had entered the chamber, the lady fell at his feet and embraced him closely, begging his pardon for her crime. He had no part in this affair. 'Lady,' he said, 'what are you saying? There is nothing but good between us. Whatever you wish, let it be pardoned! Tell me your will!' 'Lord, since you have forgiven me, listen to what I have to tell you! Once, in my great wickedness, I slandered my neighbour. I spoke ill of her two children, but in fact I did myself harm. The truth is that I became with child and had two daughters, one of whom I hid. I had her abandoned at a church and sent with her our brocade and the ring you gave me when you first spoke with me. It can be hidden from you no longer: I have found the cloth and the ring, and have recognized here our daughter whom I had lost by my folly. This is the damsel, so worthy, wise and fair, whom the knight loved and whose sister he has married!' [451–84] The lord said: 'I was never as happy as I am now that we have found our daughter. God has given us great joy rather than allowing the sin to be doubled. Daughter, come here!' The girl rejoiced when she heard the story. Her father wanted to wait no longer and went to fetch his son-in-law himself to tell him the story, taking the archbishop with him. The knight was never so joyful as when he learnt about it. The archbishop recommended that things be left as they were that night; the next day he would unjoin those he had married. Thus they agreed and the following day the two were separated. Gurun then married his beloved and her father gave her to him as a mark of affection. He gave her half his inheritance and he and her mother were present at the wedding with their other daughter, as was fitting. When they returned to their own country, they took their daughter La Codre with them. She later made a rich marriage. [485–514]

When the truth of this adventure was known, they composed the lay of *Le Fresne*. It was given this title on account of its heroine. [515–18]

IV

BISCLAVRET

In my effort to compose lays I do not wish to omit *Bisclavret* – for such is its name in Breton, while the Normans call it *Garwaf*. In days gone by one could hear tell, and indeed it often used to happen, that many men turned into werewolves and went to live in the woods. A werewolf is a ferocious beast which, when possessed by this madness, devours men, causes great damage and dwells in vast forests. I leave such matters for the moment, for I wish to tell you about Bisclavret. [1–14]

In Brittany there lived a baron whom I have heard greatly praised. He was a good and handsome knight who conducted himself nobly. He was one of his lord's closest advisers and was well loved by all his neighbours. As his wedded wife he had a woman who was worthy and attractive in appearance. He loved her and she returned his love. But one thing caused her great worry: each week he was absent for three full days without her knowing what became of him or where he went, and no one in the household knew what happened to him. One day, when he had returned home in high spirits, she questioned him: 'Lord,' she said, 'my dear, sweet love, I would gladly ask you something, if only I dared; but there is nothing I fear more than your anger.' [15–35] When he heard this, he embraced her, drew her towards him and kissed her. 'Lady,' he said, 'come, ask your question! There is nothing you can ask which I shall not tell you, if I know the answer.' 'In faith,' she said, 'I am relieved to hear this. Lord, I am so fraught with anxiety the days you are apart from me, my heart is so heavy and I have such a fear of losing you that I shall surely die shortly from this unless I soon get help. Please tell me where you go, what becomes of you and where you stay. I think you must have a lover and, if this is so, you are doing wrong.' 'Lady,' he said, 'in God's name, have mercy on me! If I tell you this, great harm will come to me, for as a result I shall lose your love and destroy myself.' [36–56]

When the lady heard what he said, she thought it was no laughing matter. She questioned him repeatedly and coaxed him so persuasively that he told her his story, keeping nothing secret. 'Lady, I become a werewolf: I enter the vast forest and live in the deepest part of the wood where I feed off the prey I can capture.' When he had related everything to her, she asked him whether he undressed or remained clothed. 'Lady,' he said, 'I go about completely naked.' 'Tell me, in the name of God, where do you leave your clothes?' 'That I will not tell you, for if I lost them and were discovered in that state, I should remain a werewolf forever. No one would be able to help me until they were returned to me. That is why I do not wish this to be known.' [57–79] 'Lord,' the lady replied to him, 'I love you more than the whole world. You must not hide anything from me or doubt me in any way. That would not seem like true love. What have I done wrong? What sin have I committed that you should doubt me in any way? Do tell me – you will be acting wisely'. She tormented and harried him so much that he could not do otherwise but tell her. 'Lady,' he said, 'beside the wood, near the path I follow, stands an old chapel which often serves me well. There beneath a bush is a broad stone, hollowed out in the centre, in which I put my clothes until I return home.' The lady heard this remarkable revelation and her face became flushed with fear. She was greatly alarmed by the story, and began to consider various means of parting from him, as she no longer wished to lie with him. [80–102] She sent a messenger to summon a knight who lived in the region and who had loved her for a long time, wooed her ardently and served her generously. She had never loved him or promised him her affection but now she told him what was on her mind. 'Friend,' she said, 'rejoice: without further delay I grant you that which has tormented you, never again will you encounter any refusal. I offer you my love and my body; make me your mistress.' He thanked her warmly and accepted her pledge, whereupon she received his oath and told him of her husband and what became of him. She described the path he took to the forest and sent him for her husband's clothes. Thus was Bisclavret betrayed and wronged by his wife. Because he was often missing, everyone thought that this time he had gone away for good. They searched and inquired for him a long while but, as no trace of him was found, they had to let the matter drop. Then the knight married the lady he had loved for so long. [103–34]

A whole year passed by until one day the king went hunting and headed straight for the forest in which Bisclavret was living. When the hounds were unleashed they came upon Bisclavret and the dogs and hunters spent the whole day in pursuit until they were just about to capture him, tear him to pieces and destroy him. As soon as he saw the king he ran up to him and begged for mercy. He took hold of his stirrup and kissed his foot and his leg. The king saw him and was filled with dread. He summoned all his companions. 'Lords,' he said, 'come forward! See the marvellous way this beast humbles itself before me! It has the intelligence of a human and is pleading for mercy. Drive back all the dogs and see that no one strikes it! The beast possesses understanding and intelligence. Hurry! Let us depart. I shall place the creature under my protection, for I shall hunt no more today.' [135–60]

The king then left with Bisclavret following him. He kept very close to the king, as he did not want to be separated from him and had no wish to abandon him. The king, who took him straight to his castle, was delighted and overjoyed at what had happened, for never before had he seen such a thing. He considered the wolf to be a great wonder and loved it dearly, commanding all his people to guard it well for love of him and not to do it any harm. None of them was to strike it and plenty of food and water must be provided for it. His men were happy to look after the creature and each day it would sleep amongst the knights, just by the king. It was loved by everyone and so noble and gentle a beast was it that it never attempted to cause any harm. Wherever the king might go, it never wanted to be left behind. It accompanied him constantly and showed clearly that it loved him. [161–84]

Now hear what happened next. The king held court and all his barons and those who held fiefs from him were summoned so that they could help him celebrate the festival and serve him all the better. Amongst them, richly and elegantly attired, was the knight who had married Bisclavret's wife. He did not realize and would never have suspected that Bisclavret was so close by. As soon as he arrived at the palace, Bisclavret caught sight of the knight and sped towards him, sinking his teeth into him and dragging him

down towards him. He would soon have done the knight serious
harm if the king had not called him and threatened him with a
stick. On two occasions that day he attempted to bite him. Many
people were greatly astonished at this for never before had he
shown signs of such behaviour towards anyone he had seen.
Throughout the household it was remarked that he would not have
done it without good reason. The knight had wronged him somehow
or other, for he was bent on revenge. On this occasion that was the
end of the matter, until the festival came to a close and the barons
took their leave and returned home. The knight whom Bisclavret
attacked was one of the very first to go, I believe. No wonder
Bisclavret hated him. [185–218]

Not long afterwards, as I understand it, the king, who was wise
and courtly, went into the forest where Bisclavret had been dis-
covered. Bisclavret accompanied him and on the way home that
night the king took lodging in that region. Bisclavret's wife learnt
of this and, dressing herself elegantly, went next day to speak to
the king, taking an expensive present for him. When Bisclavret saw
her approach, no one could restrain him. He dashed towards her
like a madman. Just hear how successfully he took his revenge. He
tore the nose right off her face. What worse punishment could he
have inflicted on her? From all sides he was threatened and was on
the point of being torn to pieces, when a wise man said to the king:
'Lord, listen to me. This beast has lived with you and every single
one of us has seen him over a long period and has been with him at
close quarters. Never before has he touched a soul or committed a
hostile act, except against this lady here. By the faith I owe you, he
has some grudge against her and also against her husband. She is
the wife of the knight you used to love so dearly and who has been
missing for a long time without our knowing what became of him.
Question the lady to see if she will tell you why the beast hates her.
Make her tell you, if she knows! We have witnessed many marvels
happening in Brittany.' [219–60] The king accepted his advice.
Holding the knight, he took the lady away and subjected her to
torture. Pain and fear combined made her reveal everything about
her husband: how she had betrayed him and taken his clothes,
about his account of what happened, what became of him and
where he went. Since his clothes had been taken he had not been
seen in the region. She was quite convinced that the beast was

Bisclavret. The king asked her for the clothes and, whether she liked it or not, made her bring them and return them to Bisclavret. When they were placed before him, Bisclavret took no notice of them. The man who gave the advice earlier called to the king: 'Lord, you are not acting properly: nothing would induce him to put on his clothing in front of you or change his animal form. You do not realize the importance of this; it is most humiliating for him. Take him into your bedchamber and bring him the clothes. Let us leave him there for a while and we shall soon see if he turns into a man.' [261–92] The king himself led the way and closed all the doors on the wolf. After a while he returned, taking two barons with him. All three entered the room. They found the knight sleeping on the king's own bed. The king ran forward to embrace him, and kissed him many times. It was not long before he restored his land to him; he gave him more than I can tell and banished the woman from the country, exiling her from the region. The man for whom she betrayed her husband went with her. She had a good many children who were thereafter recognizable by their appearance. Many of the women in the family, I tell you truly, were born without noses and lived noseless. [293–314]

The adventure you have heard actually took place, do not doubt it. The lay was composed about Bisclavret to be remembered for ever more. [315–18]

V

LANVAL

Just as it happened, I shall relate to you the story of another lay, which tells of a very noble young man whose name in Breton is Lanval. [1–4]

Arthur, the worthy and courtly king, was at Carlisle on account of the Scots and the Picts who were ravaging the country, penetrating into the land of Logres and frequently laying it waste.

The king was there during the summer, at Pentecost, and he gave many rich gifts to counts and barons and to those of the Round Table: there was no such company in the whole world. He apportioned wives and lands to all, save to one who had served him: this was Lanval, whom he did not remember, and for whom no one put in a good word. Because of his valour, generosity, beauty and prowess, many were envious of him. There were those who pretended to hold him in esteem, but who would not have uttered a single regret if misfortune had befallen him. He was the son of a king of noble birth, but far from his inheritance, and although he belonged to Arthur's household he had spent all his wealth, for the king gave him nothing and Lanval asked for nothing. Now he was in a plight, very sad and forlorn. Lords, do not be surprised: a stranger bereft of advice can be very downcast in another land when he does not know where to seek help. [5–38]

This knight whose tale I am telling you had served the king well. One day he mounted his horse and went to take his ease. He left the town and came alone to a meadow, dismounting by a stream; but there his horse trembled violently, so he loosened its saddlegirth and left it, allowing it to enter the meadow to roll over on its back. He folded his cloak, which he placed beneath his head, very disconsolate because of his troubles, and nothing could please him. Lying thus, he looked downriver and saw two damsels coming, more beautiful than any he had ever seen: they were richly dressed in closely fitting tunics of dark purple and their faces were very beautiful. The older one carried dishes of gold, well and finely made – I will not fail to tell you the truth – and the other carried a towel. They went straight to where the knight lay and Lanval, who was very well-mannered, stood up to meet them. They first greeted him and then delivered their message: 'Sir Lanval, my damsel, who is very worthy, wise and fair, has sent us for you. Come with us, for we will conduct you safely. Look, her tent is near.' [39–76] The knight went with them, disregarding his horse which was grazing before him in the meadow. They led him to the tent, which was so beautiful and well-appointed that neither Queen Semiramis at the height of her wealth, power and knowledge, nor the Emperor Octavian, could have afforded even the right-hand side of it. There was a golden eagle placed on the top, the value of which I cannot tell, nor of the ropes or the poles which supported the walls of the tent. There is no king under the sun who could afford it, however much he might give. Inside this tent was the maiden who surpassed in beauty the lily and the new rose when it appears in summer. She lay on a very beautiful bed – the coverlets cost as much as a castle – clad only in her shift. Her body was well formed and handsome, and in order to protect herself from the heat of the sun, she had cast about her a costly mantle of white ermine covered with Alexandrian purple. Her side, though, was uncovered, as well as her face, neck and breast; she was whiter than the hawthorn blossom. [77–106]

The maiden called the knight, who came forward and sat before the bed. 'Lanval,' she said, 'fair friend, for you I came from my country. I have come far in search of you and if you are worthy and courtly, no emperor, count or king will have felt as much joy or happiness as you, for I love you above all else.' He looked at her and saw that she was beautiful. Love's spark pricked him so that his heart was set alight, and he replied to her in seemly manner: 'Fair lady, if it were to please you to grant me the joy of wanting to love me, you could ask nothing that I would not do as best I could, be it foolish or wise. I shall do as you bid and abandon all others for you. I never want to leave you and this is what I most desire.' When the girl heard these words from the man who loved her so, she granted him her love and her body. Now Lanval was on the right path! She gave him a boon, that henceforth he could wish for nothing which he would not have, and however generously he gave or spent, she would still find enough for him. Lanval was very well lodged, for the more he spent, the more gold and silver he would have. 'Beloved,' she said, 'I admonish, order, and beg you not to reveal this secret to anyone! I shall tell you the long and the short of it: you would lose me forever if this love were to become known. You would never be able to see me or possess me.' He replied that he would do what she commanded. [107–52] He lay down beside her on the bed: now Lanval was well lodged. That afternoon he remained with her until evening and would have done so longer had he been able and had his love allowed him. 'Beloved,' she said, 'arise! You can stay no longer. Go from here and I shall remain, but I shall tell you one thing: whenever you wish to speak with me, you will not be able to think of a place where a man may enjoy his love without reproach or wickedness, that I shall not be there with you to do your bidding. No man save you will see me or hear my voice.' When he heard this, Lanval was well pleased and, kissing her, he arose. The damsels who had led him to the tent dressed him in rich garments, and in his new clothes there was no more handsome young man on earth. He was neither foolish nor ill-mannered. The damsels gave him water to wash his hands and a towel to dry them and then brought him food. He took his supper, which was not to be disdained, with his beloved. He was very courteously served and dined joyfully. There was one dish in abundance that pleased the knight particularly, for he often kissed his beloved and embraced her closely. [153–88]

When they had risen from table, his horse was brought to him, well saddled. Lanval was richly served there. He took his leave, mounted, and went towards the city, often looking behind him, for he was greatly disturbed, thinking of his adventure and uneasy in his heart. He was at a loss to know what to think, for he could not believe it was true. When he came to his lodgings, he found his men finely dressed. That night he offered lavish hospitality but no one knew how this came to be. There was no knight in the town in sore need of shelter whom he did not summon and serve richly and well. Lanval gave costly gifts, Lanval freed prisoners, Lanval clothed the jongleurs, Lanval performed many honourable acts. There was no one, stranger or friend, to whom he would not have given gifts. He experienced great joy and pleasure, for day or night he could see his beloved often and she was entirely at his command. [189–218]

In the same year, I believe, after St John's day, as many as thirty knights had gone to relax in a garden beneath the tower where the queen was staying. Gawain was with them and his cousin, the fair Ywain. Gawain, the noble and the worthy, who endeared himself to all, said: 'In God's name, lords, we treat our companion Lanval ill, for he is so generous and courtly, and his father is a rich king, yet we have not brought him with us.' So they returned, went to his lodgings and persuaded him to come with them.

The queen, in the company of three ladies, was reclining by a window cut out of the stone when she caught sight of the king's household and recognized Lanval. She called one of her ladies to summon her most elegant and beautiful damsels to relax with her in the garden where the others were. She took more than thirty with her, and they went down the steps where the knights, glad of their coming, came to meet them. They took the girls by the hand and the conversation was not uncourtly. [219–52] Lanval withdrew to one side, far from the others, for he was impatient to hold his beloved, to kiss, embrace and touch her. He cared little for other people's joy when he could not have his own pleasure. When the queen saw the knight alone, she approached him straightaway. Sitting down beside him, she spoke to him and opened her heart. 'Lanval, I have honoured, cherished and loved you much. You may have all my love: just tell me what you desire! I grant you my love and you should be glad to have me.' 'Lady,' he said, 'leave me be! I have no desire to love you, for I have long served the king and do not want to betray my faith. Neither you nor your love will ever lead me to wrong my lord!' The queen became angry and distressed, and spoke unwisely: 'Lanval,' she said, 'I well believe that you do not like this kind of pleasure. I have been told often enough that you have no desire for women. You have well-trained young men and enjoy yourself with them. Base coward, wicked recreant, my lord is extremely unfortunate to have suffered you near him. I think he may have lost his salvation because of it!' [253–86]

When he heard her, he was distressed, but not slow to reply. He said something in spite that he was often to regret. 'Lady, I am not skilled in the profession you mention, but I love and am loved by a lady who should be prized above all others I know. And I will tell you one thing: you can be sure that one of her servants, even the very poorest girl, is worth more than you, my lady the Queen, in body, face and beauty, wisdom and goodness.' Thereupon the queen left and went in tears to her chamber, very distressed and angry that he had humiliated her in this way. She took to her bed ill and said that she would never again get up, unless the king saw that justice was done her in respect of her complaint. [287–310]

The king had returned from the woods after an extremely happy day. He entered the queen's apartments and when she saw him, she complained aloud, fell at his feet, cried for mercy and said that Lanval had shamed her. He had requested her love and because she had refused him, had insulted and deeply humiliated her. He had boasted of a beloved who was so well-bred, noble and proud that her chambermaid, the poorest servant she had, was worthier than the queen. The king grew very angry and swore on oath that, if Lanval could not defend himself in court, he would have him burned or hanged. The king left the room, summoned three of his barons and sent them for Lanval, who was suffering great pain. He had returned to his lodgings, well aware of having lost his beloved by revealing their love. Alone in his chamber, distraught and anguished, he called his beloved repeatedly, but to no avail. He lamented and sighed, fainting from time to time; a hundred times he cried to her to have mercy, to come and speak with her beloved. He cursed his heart and his mouth and it was a wonder he did not kill himself. His cries and moans were not loud enough nor his agitation and torment such that she would have mercy on him, or even permit him to see her. Alas, what will he do? [311–51]

The king's men arrived and told Lanval to go to court without delay: the king had summoned him through them, for the queen had accused him. Lanval went sorrowfully and would have been happy for them to kill him. He came before the king, sad, subdued and silent, betraying his great sorrow. The king said to him angrily: 'Vassal, you have wronged me greatly! You were extremely ill-advised to shame and vilify me, and to slander the queen. You boasted out of folly, for your beloved must be very noble for her handmaiden to be more beautiful and more worthy than the queen.' [352–70]

Lanval denied point by point having offended and shamed his

lord, and maintained that he had not sought the queen's love, but he acknowledged the truth of his words about the love of which he had boasted. He now regretted this, for as a result he had lost her. He told them he would do whatever the court decreed in this matter, but the king was very angry and sent for all his men to tell him exactly what he should do, so that his action would not be unfavourably interpreted. Whether they liked it or not, they obeyed his command and assembled to make a judgement, deciding that a day should be fixed for the trial, but that Lanval should provide his lord with pledges that he would await his judgement and return later to his presence. Then the court would be larger, for at that moment only the king's household itself was present. The barons returned to the king and explained their reasoning. The king asked for pledges, but Lanval was alone and forlorn, having no relation or friend there. Then Gawain approached and offered to stand bail, and all his companions did likewise. The king said to them: 'I entrust him to you on surety of all that you hold from me, lands and fiefs, each man separately.' When this had been pledged, there was no more to be done, and Lanval returned to his lodging with the knights escorting him. They chastised him and urged him strongly not to be so sorrowful, and cursed such foolish love. They went to see him every day, as they wished to know whether he was drinking and eating properly, being very much afraid that he might harm himself. [371–414]

On the appointed day the barons assembled. The king and queen were there and the guarantors brought Lanval to court. They were all very sad on his account and I think there were a hundred who would have done all in their power to have him released without a trial because he had been wrongly accused. The king demanded the verdict according to the charge and the rebuttal, and now everything lay in the hands of the barons. They considered their judgement, very troubled and concerned on account of this noble man from abroad, who was in such a plight in their midst. Some of them wanted to harm him in conformity with their lord's will. [415–32] Thus spoke the Count of Cornwall: 'There shall be no default on our part. Like it or not, right must prevail. The king accused his vassal, whom I heard you call Lanval, of a felony and charged him with a crime, about a love he boasted of which angered my lady. Only the king is accusing him, so by the faith I owe you, there ought, to tell the truth, to be no case to answer, were it not that one should honour one's lord in all things. An oath will bind Lanval and the king will put the matter in our hands. If he can provide proof and his beloved comes forward, and if what he said to incur the queen's displeasure is true, then he will be pardoned, since he did not say it to spite her. And if he cannot furnish proof, then we must inform him that he will lose the king's service and that the king must banish him.' They sent word to the knight and informed him that he should send for his beloved to defend and protect him. He told them that this was not possible and that he would receive no help from her. The messengers returned to the judges, expecting no help to be forthcoming for Lanval. The king pressed them hard because the queen was waiting for them. [433–70]

When they were about to give their verdict, they saw two maidens approaching on two fine ambling palfreys. They were extremely comely and dressed only in purple taffeta, next to their bare skin; the knights were pleased to see them. Gawain and three other knights went to Lanval, told him about this, and pointed the two maidens out to him. Gawain was very glad and strongly urged Lanval to tell him if this was his beloved, but he told them that he did not know who they were, whence they came or where they were going. The maidens continued to approach, still on horseback, and then dismounted before the dais where King Arthur was seated. They were of great beauty and spoke in courtly fashion: 'King, make your chambers available and hang them with silken curtains so that my lady may stay here, for she wishes to lodge with you.' This he granted them willingly and summoned two knights who led them to the upper chambers. For the moment they said no more. [471–98]

The king asked his barons for the judgement and the responses, and said that they had greatly angered him by the long delay. 'Lord,' they said, 'we are deliberating, but because of the ladies we saw, we have not reached a verdict. Let us continue with the trial.' So they assembled in some anxiety, and there was a good deal of commotion and contention. [499–508]

While they were in this troubled state, they saw two finely accoutred maidens coming along the street, dressed in garments of Phrygian silk and riding on Spanish mules. The vassals were glad of this and they said to each other that Lanval, the worthy and brave, was now saved. Ywain went up to him with his companions, and said: 'Lord, rejoice! For the love of God, speak to us! Two damsels are approaching, very comely and beautiful. It is surely your beloved.' Lanval quickly replied that he did not recognize them, nor did he know or love them. When they had arrived, they dismounted before the king and many praised them highly for their bodies, faces, and complexions. They were both more worthy than the queen had ever been. The older of the two, who was courtly and wise, delivered her message fittingly: 'King, place your chambers at our disposal for the purpose of lodging my lady. She is coming here to speak with you.' He ordered them to be taken to the others who had arrived earlier. They paid no heed to their mules, and, as soon as they had left the king, he summoned all his barons so that they might deliver their verdict. This had taken up too much of the day and the queen, who had been waiting for them for such a long time, was getting angry. [509–46]

Just as they were about to give their verdict, a maiden on horseback entered the town. There was none more beautiful in the whole world. She was riding a white palfrey which carried her well and gently; its neck and head were well-formed and there was no finer animal on earth. The palfrey was richly equipped, for no count or king on earth could have paid for it, save by selling or pledging his lands. The lady was dressed in a white tunic and shift, laced left and right so as to reveal her sides. Her body was comely, her hips low, her neck whiter than snow on a branch; her eyes were bright and her face white, her mouth fair and her nose well-placed; her eyebrows were brown and her brow fair, and her hair curly and rather blond. A golden thread does not shine as brightly as the rays reflected in the light from her hair. Her cloak was of dark silk and she had wrapped its skirts about her. She held a sparrowhawk on her wrist and behind her there followed a dog. There was no one in the town, humble or powerful, old or young, who did not watch her arrival, and no one jested about her beauty. She approached slowly and the judges who saw her thought it was a great wonder. No one who had looked at her could have failed to be inspired with real joy. [547–84] Those who loved the knight went and told him about the maiden who was coming and who, please God, would deliver him. 'Lord and friend, here comes a lady whose hair is neither tawny nor brown. She is the most beautiful of all women in the world.' Lanval heard this and raised his head, for he knew her well, and sighed. His blood rushed to his face and he was quick to speak: 'In faith,' he said, 'it is my beloved! If she shows me no mercy, I hardly care if anyone should kill me, for my cure is in seeing her.' The lady entered the palace, where no one so beautiful had ever before been seen. She dismounted before the king, and in the sight of all, let her cloak fall so that they could see her better. The king, who was well-mannered, rose to meet her, and all the others honoured her and offered themselves as her servants. [585–610] When they had looked at her and praised her beauty greatly, she spoke thus, for she had no wish to remain: 'King, I have loved one of your vassals, Lanval, whom you see there. Because of what he said, he was accused in your court, and I do not wish him to come to any harm. You should know that the queen was wrong, as he never sought her love. As regards the boast he made, if he can be acquitted by me, let your barons release him!' The king granted that it should be as the judges recommended, in accordance with justice. There was not one who did not consider that Lanval had successfully defended himself, and so he was freed by their decision. The maiden, who had many servants, then left, for the king could not retain her. Outside the hall there was a large block of dark marble on to which heavily armed men climbed when they left the king's court. Lanval mounted it and when the maiden came through the door, he leapt in a single bound on to the palfrey behind her. He went with her to Avalon, so the Bretons tell us, to a very beautiful island. Thither the young man was borne and no one has heard any more about him, nor can I relate any more. [611–46]

VI

LES DEUS AMANZ

There once took place in Normandy a now celebrated adventure of two young people who loved each other and who both met their end because of love. The Bretons made a lay about them which was given the title *The Two Lovers*. [1–6]

The truth is that in Neustria, which we call Normandy, there is a marvellously high mountain where the two young people lie. Near this mountain, on one side, a king, who was lord of the Pistrians, wisely and carefully had a city built which he named after the inhabitants and called Pitres. The name has survived to this day and there is still a town and houses there. We know the area well, for it is called the Valley of Pitres. The king had a beautiful daughter, a most courtly damsel who had been a comfort to him ever since he had lost the queen. Many people reproached him for this, and even his own people blamed him. When he heard that people were talking thus, he was very sad and disturbed, and began to consider how he could prevent anyone seeking his daughter's hand. Far and near he had it proclaimed that whoever wanted to win his daughter ought to know one thing for certain: that it was decreed and destined that he should carry her in his arms, without resting, up the mountain outside the town. When the news was known and had spread throughout the region, many made the attempt, but without success. There were some who made such an effort that they carried the girl halfway up the mountain, but could go no further and had to abandon the attempt. She remained unmarried for a long time, as no one wanted to seek her hand. [7–48]

There was in the country a young man, noble and fair, the son of a count. He strove to perform well so as to be esteemed above all others and he frequented the king's court and often stayed there. He fell in love with the king's daughter and many times urged her to grant him her love and to love him truly. Because he was worthy and courtly, and because the king held him in high esteem, she granted him her love for which he humbly thanked her. They often spoke together and loved each other loyally, concealing their love as best they could so that no one would notice them. This suffering caused them much grief, but the young man considered it better to suffer these misfortunes than to make too much haste and thus fail. Love was a great affliction to him. Then once it happened that the young man, so wise, worthy and fair, came to his beloved and addressed his complaint to her, begging her in his anguish to elope with him, for he could no longer bear the pain. He knew full well that her father loved her so much that, if he asked for her, she would not be given to him unless he could carry her in his arms to the top of the mountain. [49–83] The damsel answered him: 'Beloved, I know it is impossible for you to carry me, for you are not strong enough. But if I went away with you, my father would be sad and distressed and his life would be an endless torment. Truly, I love him so much and hold him so dear that I would not wish to grieve him. You must decide upon something else, for I will not hear of this. I have a relative in Salerno, a rich woman with a large income, who has been there for more than thirty years and who has practised the art of physic so much that she is well-versed in medicines. She knows so much about herbs and roots that if you go to her, taking with you a letter from me, and tell her your story, she will give thought and consideration to the matter. She will give you such electuaries and such potions as will revive you and increase your strength. When you come back to this country, ask my father for me. He will consider you a child and tell you about the agreement whereby he will give me to no one, however hard he tries, unless he can carry me up the mountain in his arms without resting.' The young man listened to the maiden's words and advice which brought him great joy and he thanked his beloved, asking her for leave to depart. [84–120]

He went back to his homeland and quickly equipped himself with rich clothes and money, palfreys and pack-horses. Taking his most trusted men with him, the young man went to stay at Salerno and speak with his beloved's aunt. He gave her a letter from the girl and, when she had read it from start to finish, she retained him with her until she knew all about him. She fortified him with medicines and gave him a potion such that, however weary, afflicted, or burdened he might be, it would refresh his whole body, even his veins and his bones, and restore all his strength to him as soon as he had drunk it. Then he put the potion in a vessel and took it back to his land. [121–42]

On his return the young man, joyful and happy, did not stay long in his own region. He went and asked the king for his daughter, saying that if he would give her to him, he would take her and carry her up to the top of the mountain. The king did not refuse him, but still considered it great folly as he was so young, and as so many valiant, wise, and worthy men had made the attempt unsuccessfully. He named the day, summoning his vassals, his friends, and all those available to him, letting no one remain behind. People came from far and wide because of the young girl and the young man who would attempt to carry her up to the top of the mountain. The damsel made ready, fasting and refraining from eating in order to lose weight, for she wished to help her beloved. On the day everyone assembled, the young man, who had not forgotten his potion, arrived first. The king led his daughter into the meadow towards the Seine, where a great crowd gathered. She wore nothing but her shift, and the young man took her in his arms. The little phial containing the potion (he well knew that she had no wish to let him down) was given to her to carry, but I fear it will be of little avail to him, because he knew no moderation. [143–79] He set off with her at a good pace and climbed the mountain half way. She brought him such great happiness that he did not remember his potion, and when she realized he was tiring, she said: 'My love, please drink. I know you are tiring, so recover your strength.' The young man replied: 'Fair one, I feel my heart to be strong. Providing I can still walk three paces, on no account shall I stop, not even long enough to take a drink. These people would shout at us and deafen me with their noise, and they could easily distract me. I shall not stop here.' When he had climbed two thirds of the way, he nearly collapsed. The girl repeatedly begged him: 'My love, drink your potion.' Yet he would take no heed of her, and carried her onward in great pain. He reached the top, in such distress that he fell down and never rose again, for his heart left his body. The maiden saw her beloved and, thinking he had fainted, knelt down beside him and tried to make him drink. But he could not speak to her. Thus he died, just as I am telling you. She lamented him loudly and then threw away the vessel containing the potion, scattering its contents so that the mountain was well sprinkled with it, and the land and surrounding area much improved. Many good plants were found there which took root because of the potion. [180–219]

Now I shall tell you about the girl: because she had lost her beloved, she was more distressed than ever before. She lay down beside him, took him in her arms and embraced him, kissing his eyes and his mouth repeatedly. Sorrow for him touched her heart and there this damsel died, who was so worthy, wise and fair. When the king and those who were waiting saw that they were not coming, they went after them and found them. The king fell to the ground in a swoon, and when he could speak, he lamented loudly, as did all the strangers. They left them there on the ground for three days, and then had a marble coffin brought and the two young people placed in it. On the advice of those present they buried them on top of the mountain and then departed.[220–40]

Because of what happened to these two young people, the mountain is called The Mountain of the Two Lovers. The events took place just as I have told you, and the Bretons composed a lay about them. [241–4]

VII

YONEC

Now that I have begun to compose lays, I shall not cease my effort but shall relate fully in rhyme the adventures that I know. It is my intention and desire henceforth to tell you about Yonec, under what circumstances he was born and how his father, whose name was Muldumarec, first met his mother. [1–10]

In Britain there once lived a rich old man who held the fief of Caerwent and was acknowledged lord of the land.[1] The city lay on the River Duelas and formerly ships could reach it. This man was very old and, because his inheritance would be large, he took a wife in order to have children, who would be his heirs. The maiden who was given to the rich man was from a noble family, wise, courtly and extremely beautiful. He loved her greatly on account of her beauty, but because she was so fair and noble, he took good care to watch over her and locked her in his tower in a large paved chamber. He had a sister, old and widowed, without a husband, and he placed her with the lady to keep her from going astray. There were other women, I believe, in a separate room, but the lady would never have spoken to them without the old woman's permission. [11–36]

Thus he held her for seven years – they never had any children – and she did not leave the tower either for family or friend. When the lord went to bed, there was neither chamberlain nor door-keeper who would have dared enter the chamber to light a candle before him. The lady was in great distress, and she wept and sighed so much that she lost her beauty, as happens to any woman who fails to take care of herself. She would herself have preferred death to take her quickly.

It was the beginning of the month of April, when the birds sing their songs, that the lord arose in the early morning and prepared to set out for the woods. He had made the old woman get up and lock the doors after him. When she had done his bidding, he left with his men. The old woman carried her psalter from which she intended to recite psalms. [37–59] The lady lay awake weeping and looking at the sunlight. She noticed that the old woman had left the room and grieved, sighed and lamented tearfully: 'Alas,' she said, 'that ever I was born! My destiny is hard indeed. I am a prisoner in this tower and death alone will free me. What is this jealous old man afraid of, to keep me so securely imprisoned? He is extremely stupid and foolish, always fearing that he will be betrayed. I can neither go to church nor hear God's service. I could put on a friendly mien for him, even without any desire to do so, if I could talk to people and join them in amusement. Cursed be my parents and all those who gave me to this jealous man and married me to his person! I pull and tug on a strong rope! He will never die. When he should have been baptized, he was plunged into the river of Hell, for his sinews are hard, and so are his veins which are full of living blood. I have often heard tell that in this country one used to encounter adventures which relieved those afflicted by care: knights discovered maidens to their liking, noble and fair, and ladies found handsome and courtly lovers, worthy and valiant men. There was no fear of reproach and they alone could see them. If this can be and ever was, if it ever did happen to anyone, may almighty God grant my wish!' [60–104]

Having lamented thus, she noticed the shadow of a large bird through a narrow window, but did not know what it could be. The bird flew into the room: it had straps on its feet and looked like a hawk of five or six moultings. It landed before the lady, and after it had been there for a while for her to see, it turned into a fair and noble knight. The lady was astounded by this. Her face became flushed, and she trembled and covered her head, being very afraid. The knight was extremely courtly and spoke to her first: 'Lady, do not be afraid! The hawk is a noble bird. Even if its secrets remain a mystery to you, be assured that you are safe, and make me your beloved! This is the reason I came here. I have loved you for a long time and desired you greatly in my heart. I never loved any woman but you, nor shall I ever love another. Yet I could not come to you, nor leave my country, unless you had wished for me; but now I can be your beloved!' The lady, now assured, uncovered her head and spoke. She answered the knight, saying that she would make him her lover, provided he believed in God, which would make their love possible. He was very handsome and never in her life had she seen such a handsome knight, nor would she ever again. [105–44] 'Lady,' he said, 'you are right. I would not on any account want guilt, distrust or suspicion to attach to me. I do believe in the Creator who set us free from the sorrow in which our ancestor Adam put us by biting the bitter apple. He is, will be and always has been life and light to sinners. If you do not believe this of me, send for your chaplain. Tell him that an illness has come upon you and that you want to hear the service that God has established in this world for the redemption of sinners. I shall assume your appearance, receive the body of Christ, and recite all of my credo for you. Never doubt me on this count.' She replied that he had spoken well. He lay down next to her on the bed, but did not intend to touch, embrace or kiss her. Then the old woman returned, and when she found the lady awake she told her it was time to get up and that she would bring her clothes. The lady said that she was ill and she must ensure that the chaplain came quickly to her, for she was very much afraid of dying. The old woman said: 'Be patient now! My lord has gone to the woods. No one but me may enter here.' The lady was very afraid and pretended to faint, and when the old woman saw her she was greatly alarmed. She opened the door of the chamber and sent for the priest, who came as quickly as possible, bringing the *corpus domini*. The knight received it and drank the wine from the chalice, whereupon the chaplain left and the old woman closed the doors. [145–90]

The lady lay next to her beloved: I never saw so fair a couple. When they had laughed and sported and exchanged confidences, the knight took his leave, for he wanted to return to his own country. She begged him gently to come back and see her often. 'Lady,' he said, 'whenever it pleases you, I shall be with you within the hour, but observe moderation so that we are not discomfited. This old woman will betray us and keep watch over us night and day. When she notices our love, she will tell her lord about it. If this should happen as I say and we are betrayed in this way, I shall have no way of preventing my death.' [191–210]

Thereupon the knight departed and left his beloved in great joy. The next day she arose quite recovered and was very happy that week. She looked after herself well and her beauty was quite restored. Now she was more content just to remain where she was than to amuse herself in any other way, for she wanted to see her beloved often and to take her pleasure with him as soon as her lord left. Night and day, early or late, he was hers whenever she wanted. Now may she, with God's grace, long enjoy her love! The great joy she often experienced on seeing her lover caused her appearance to alter. Her husband was very cunning and noticed that she was different from her usual self. He was suspicious of his sister, but spoke to her one day and said that he was astonished that the lady attired herself thus, asking what this might mean. The old woman replied that she did not know, for no one could speak to her nor did she have a friend or beloved, except that she had noticed that she remained alone more willingly than before. The lord then replied: 'In faith, that I believe! Now you must do something: in the morning when I have got up and you have locked the doors, pretend to go outside and leave her to lie alone. Stay in a secret place and watch to see what it can be that keeps her so joyful.' With this plan they parted. Alas! how ill-served were they on whom he wanted to spy in order to betray and trap them. [211–56]

Three days later, I heard tell, the lord pretended to leave, telling his wife that the king had summoned him by letter, but that he would soon be back. He then left the chamber and closed the door. The old woman arose and hid behind a curtain from where it was easy for her to hear and satisfy her curiosity. The lady lay there without sleeping, for she greatly desired her beloved who came without delay, in no time at all. They were full of joy to be with each other, to talk and exchange glances, until it was time to get up, for then the knight had to go. The old woman saw and took note of how he came and went, but was very much afraid because she saw him one moment a man and another a hawk. When the lord, who had not been far away, returned, she explained the truth about the knight. He was most distressed by this and quickly made traps to kill the knight. He had large iron spikes forged and the tips more sharply pointed than any razor. When he had prepared and cut barbs in them, he set them on the window, close together and well-positioned, in the place through which the knight passed whenever he came to see the lady. Oh God! if only he had known the treachery that the villain was preparing. [257–96]

The next morning the lord arose before daybreak and said that he intended to go hunting. The old woman went to see him off and then returned to bed, for dawn was not yet visible. The lady was awake, waiting for the man she loved faithfully, and said that he could now come and be with her quite at leisure. When she summoned him, he left without delay and flew through the window, but the spikes were in front of it. One of them pierced his body and the red blood flowed out. When he realized that he was mortally wounded, he freed himself from the prongs and entered. He sat down on the bed beside the lady, covering all the sheets in blood, and when she saw the blood and the wound she was grievously alarmed. He said to her: 'My sweet beloved, for love of you I am losing my life. I told you what would come of it: your appearance would slay us.' When she heard this, she fell into a swoon, and for a while seemed dead. He comforted her tenderly, saying that grief was of no avail, and telling her she was with child by him and would have a worthy and valiant son to comfort her. She was to call him Yonec, and he would avenge both of them and kill his enemy. [297–332]

He could remain no longer, for his wound was bleeding continuously, and he left in great pain, with her following him with loud cries. She escaped through a window, but it was a wonder she did not kill herself, for she had to jump a good twenty feet. Naked but for her shift, she followed the trail of blood which flowed from the knight on to the path she was taking and to which she kept until she came to a hill. In this hill there was an opening, all covered in his blood, but she could see nothing beyond and therefore assumed that her beloved had entered there. She hurriedly went in, but finding no light, followed the straight path until she emerged on the other side of the hill, in a beautiful meadow. She found the grass wet with blood, which alarmed her greatly, and followed the trail through the meadow. [333–59] There was a city nearby, completely enclosed by a wall, where there was not a house, hall or tower which did not seem to be made of solid silver. The state rooms were especially rich. Over towards the town were the marshes, the forests and the enclosures, and in the other direction, towards the keep, a stream flowed all around, where the ships used to arrive, and there were more than three hundred sails. Downstream the gate was unlocked, and so the lady entered the town, still following the fresh blood through the centre of the town up to the castle. No one at all spoke to her, for she encountered neither man nor woman. She came to the paved entrance of the palace and found it covered in blood, and when she went into a beautiful chamber she found a knight sleeping, but did not recognize him and continued into another, larger, room. There, finding nothing but a bed with a knight sleeping on it, she passed through. She entered the third room and found her beloved's bed. The bedposts were of pure gold, and I cannot estimate the worth of the bedclothes. The candles and the candelabra, lit by both night and day, were worth all the gold in an entire city. [360–92] As soon as she saw the knight she recognized him, and approached in alarm, falling over him in a swoon. He who loved her deeply took her in his arms and lamented his misfortune repeatedly. When she had recovered, he comforted her gently: 'Fair beloved, in God's name, have mercy! Go away! Flee from here! I shall die soon, before daybreak. There would be such grief here if you were found, and you would be tormented, for my people would know that they had lost me because of my love for you. I am sad and troubled for your sake.' The lady said to him: 'Beloved, I should rather die together with you than suffer with my husband. If I go back to him, he will kill me.' The knight reassured her, gave her a ring, and told her that as long as she kept it her husband would remember nothing that had happened and would not keep her in custody. He gave and commended to her his sword, then enjoined her to prevent any man from ever taking possession of it, but to keep it for the use of her son. [393–424] When he had grown up and become a worthy and valiant knight, she should take him and her husband to a feast. They would come to an abbey and at a tomb they would visit, they would again hear about his death and how he was unjustly killed. There she would give the sword to his son who was to be told the story of his birth and who his father was. Then they would see what he would do. When he had explained everything to her, he gave her a costly tunic, and ordered her to put it on. Then he made her leave him, and she went away wearing the ring and carrying the sword that comforted her. She had not gone half a league from the city when she heard the bells ringing and the lamentation in the castle. She swooned four times with grief and, when she recovered, made her way towards the hill, which she passed through and arrived back in her own region. She remained afterwards a long time together with her husband, who made no accusations against her, and neither slandered nor mocked her. [425–56]

Their son was born and well brought up, well protected and well loved. They called him Yonec and in the whole kingdom there was not a fairer, worthier, more valiant or more generous man to be found. When he had come of age, they had him dubbed a knight, but now listen to what happened that same year!

As was the custom of the country the lord had been summoned with his friends to the feast of St Aaron, which was celebrated in Caerleon and in several other cities. He took his wife and son and dressed himself richly; so it was that they set out, not knowing exactly where they were going. With them was a young lad who led them along the straight road until they came to a castle, fairer than any other in the whole world. Inside there was an abbey with very holy people, where the squire who was taking them to the feast found them lodgings. They were well served and honoured in the abbot's chamber, and next morning went to hear mass. Then they intended to leave, but the abbot came to talk to them and begged them to stay, for he wanted to show them his dormitory, his chapter-house and his refectory, and since they were well-lodged, the lord consented to stay. [457–92]

That day after dinner they visited the various rooms. First they came to the chapter-house where they found a great tomb covered with a cloth of striped brocade with a band of rich gold material running through it. At the head, feet and sides, there were twenty lighted candles. The candelabra were of fine gold, and the censers which were used by day to honour the tomb with fragrance, of amethyst. They inquired of the inhabitants whose tomb it was and who lay there. At this, the inhabitants began to weep and said amidst their tears that it was the best knight, the strongest and the fiercest, the fairest and the most beloved, who had ever been born. He had been king of that land and none had ever been as courtly. He had been destroyed at Caerwent and killed for the love of a lady [493–520]: 'We have never since had a lord, but, just as he said and commanded, we have waited long for a son he gave the lady.' When the lady heard this news, she called aloud to her son: 'Fair son, you have heard how God has brought us here! It is your father who lies here, whom this old man unjustly killed. Now I commend and hand over to you his sword, for I have kept it long enough.' For all to hear, she revealed to him that this was his father and he his son, how he used to come to her and how her husband had betrayed him. She told him the truth, fell into a faint on the tomb, and, while unconscious, died. She never spoke again, but when her son saw she was dead, he struck off his stepfather's head, and thus with his father's sword avenged his mother's grief. When what had happened became known throughout the city, they took the lady in great honour and laid her in the tomb. Before leaving this place they made Yonec their lord. [521–50]

Those who heard this story long afterwards composed a lay from it, about the sorrow and grief that they suffered for love. [551–4]

VIII

LAÜSTIC

I shall relate an adventure to you from which the Bretons composed a lay. *Laüstic* is its name, I believe, and that is what the Bretons call it in their land. In French the title is *Rossignol*, and Nightingale is the correct English word. [1–6]

In the region of St Malo was a famous town and two knights dwelt there, each with a fortified house. Because of the fine qualities of the two men the town acquired a good reputation. One of the knights had taken a wise, courtly and elegant wife who conducted herself, as custom dictated, with admirable propriety. The other knight was a young man who was well known amongst his peers for his prowess and great valour. He performed honourable deeds gladly and attended many tournaments, spending freely and giving generously whatever he had. He loved his neighbour's wife and so persistently did he request her love, so frequent were his entreaties and so many qualities did he possess that she loved him above all things, both for the good she had heard about him and because he lived close by. They loved each other prudently and well, concealing their love carefully to ensure that they were not seen, disturbed or suspected. This they could do because their dwellings were adjoining. Their houses, halls and keeps were close by each other and there was no barrier or division, apart from a high wall of dark-hued stone. When she stood at her bedroom window, the lady could talk to her beloved in the other house and he to her, and they could toss gifts to each other. There was scarcely anything to displease them and they were both very content except for the fact that they could not meet and take their pleasure with each other, for the lady was closely guarded when her husband was in the region. But they were so resourceful that day or night they managed to speak to each other and no one could prevent their coming to the window and seeing each other there. [7–56] For a long time they loved each other, until one summer

when the copses and meadows were green and the gardens in full
bloom. On the flower-tops the birds sang joyfully and sweetly. If
love is on anyone's mind, no wonder he turns his attention towards
it. I shall tell you the truth about the knight. Both he and the lady
made the greatest possible effort with their words and with their
eyes. At night, when the moon was shining and her husband was
asleep, she often rose from beside him and put on her mantle.
Knowing her beloved would be doing the same, she would go and
stand at the window and stay awake most of the night. They took
delight in seeing each other, since they were denied anything more.
But so frequently did she stand there and so frequently leave her
bed that her husband became angry and asked her repeatedly
why she got up and where she went. 'Lord,' replied the lady,
'anyone who does not hear the song of the nightingale knows none
of the joys of this world. This is why I come and stand here. So
sweet is the song I hear by night that it brings me great pleasure. I
take such delight in it and desire it so much that I can get no sleep
at all.' [57–90] When the lord heard what she said, he gave a
spiteful, angry laugh and devised a plan to ensnare the nightingale.
Every single servant in his household constructed some trap, net
or snare and then arranged them throughout the garden. There
was no hazel tree or chestnut tree on which they did not place a
snare or bird-lime, until they had captured and retained it. When
they had taken the nightingale, it was handed over, still alive, to
the lord, who was overjoyed to hold it in his hands. He entered the
lady's chamber. 'Lady,' he said, 'where are you? Come forward
and speak to us. With bird-lime I have trapped the nightingale
which has kept you awake so much. Now you can sleep in peace,
for it will never awaken you again.' When the lady heard him she
was grief-stricken and distressed. She asked her husband for the
bird, but he killed it out of spite, breaking its neck wickedly with
his two hands. He threw the body at the lady, so that the front of
her tunic was bespattered with blood, just on her breast. There-
upon he left the chamber. [91–120] The lady took the tiny corpse,
wept profusely and cursed those who had betrayed the nightingale
by constructing the traps and snares, for they had taken so much
joy from her. 'Alas,' she said, 'misfortune is upon me. Never again
can I get up at night or go to stand at the window where I used to
see my beloved. I know one thing for certain. He will think I am

faint-hearted, so I must take action. I shall send him the nightingale and let him know what has happened.' She wrapped the little bird in a piece of samite, embroidered in gold and covered in designs. She called one of her servants, entrusted him with her message and sent him to her beloved. He went to the knight, greeted him on behalf of his lady, related the whole message to him and presented him with the nightingale. When the messenger had finished speaking, the knight, who had listened attentively, was distressed by what had happened. But he was not uncourtly or tardy. He had a small vessel prepared, not of iron or steel, but of pure gold with fine stones, very precious and valuable. On it he carefully placed a lid and put the nightingale in it. Then he had the casket sealed and carried it with him at all times. [121–56]

This adventure was related and could not long be concealed. The Bretons composed a lay about it which is called *Laüstic*. [157–60]

IX

MILUN

Anyone who intends to present a new story must approach the problem in a new way and speak so persuasively that the tale brings pleasure to people. I shall now begin *Milun* and explain in a few words for what reason and under what conditions the lay which bears this name was composed. [1-8]

Milun was born in South Wales. From the day he was dubbed a knight he did not encounter a single knight who could unhorse him. He was an exceedingly fine knight, noble and bold, courtly and fierce. He was widely known in Ireland, Norway, Gotland, England and Scotland. Many people envied him, but he was much loved for his prowess and honoured by many princes. In the region where he lived there was a nobleman whose name I do not know. He had a beautiful daughter, a most courtly damsel. She heard Milun's name mentioned and conceived a deep love for him. She sent a messenger to tell him that, if he wished, she would be his love. Milun was delighted by this news, and thanked the damsel for her offer. He was happy to grant her his love and said he would always remain true to her. The reply he made to her was most courtly. He gave generously to the messenger and promised him sincere friendship. 'Friend,' he said, 'try to arrange for me to speak to my beloved and see to it that our secret is safe. You will take her my gold ring and give her this message on my behalf: when it pleases her, come for me and I shall go with you.' The messenger took his leave and set off. He returned to his mistress, gave her the ring and said that he had done what had been asked of him. [9-42] The damsel was full of joy because of the love thus granted to her. Milun and she frequently arranged a meeting in a garden in which she took her ease, close to her bedchamber. Milun visited the damsel so often and loved her so much that she became pregnant. When she realized this, she summoned Milun and bemoaned her fate. She told him what had happened: she had forfeited her honour and good name by allowing such a thing to befall her. She would be severely punished: tortured, or sold as a slave in another country. Such was the custom of our ancestors, still observed at that time. Milun replied that he would do whatever she suggested. 'When the child is born,' she said, 'you will take it to my married sister in Northumbria, a rich, worthy and wise lady. You will inform her in writing and by word of mouth that this is her sister's child which has already caused her much suffering. She should now see that it is properly brought up, whatever it is, boy or girl. I shall hang your ring round its neck and send her a letter. In it will be its father's name, and the story of its mother's misfortune. When it is fully grown and has reached the age of reason, she should give the child the letter and the ring. Let her command the child to keep them until it has been able to find its father.' [43–86]

They followed her plan until the time came when the damsel gave birth. An old woman, who looked after her and to whom she had told the whole story, concealed her and shielded her so well that neither by word or by outward sign was her condition discovered. The girl had a very fine son. They hung around the child's neck the ring, a silk purse, and then the letter, making sure that it could not be seen. Then they laid the child in a cradle, covered in a white linen sheet. Beneath its head they placed an expensive pillow and over the child a coverlet with a hem of marten skin. The old lady gave the child to Milun who waited in the garden and he entrusted it to loyal servants who took it away. They rested seven times a day in the towns through which they passed and fed the child, put it back to sleep and bathed it. They took a wet nurse with them: thus they displayed their loyalty. They followed the straightest path until they handed the child over to the lady, who accepted it and was happy to do so. She took the letter and the seal. When she discovered whose child it was she loved it tenderly. Those who had brought the child returned to their own country. [87–122]

Milun left his land to seek fame as a mercenary. His beloved remained at home. Her father betrothed her to a nobleman, a very wealthy man from the region, a man of great power and reputation. When she realized what was to happen to her, she was plunged into the deepest grief and often recalled Milun regretfully.

She greatly feared the consequences of having wrongfully had a child. Her husband would find out soon. 'Alas,' she said, 'what shall I do? Am I to have a husband? How can I accept him? I am no longer a virgin; I shall be a servant all my days. I never realized that things would turn out this way: I thought I could marry my beloved. We would have concealed the matter and I should never have heard it on others' lips. I would rather die than go on living. But I am not free. I have my chamberlain and many guards, young and old, who hate to see a just love and who delight in sadness. Now I shall have to suffer in this way. Oh, woe is me, that I cannot die.' When the time came for her to be given in marriage her husband took her away. [123–52]

Milun returned home. He was sad and downcast, overwhelmed by grief and sorrow. But he took heart from the fact that the girl he had loved so much lived near to his homeland. He started to work out how he could inform her, without being detected, that he had come back home. He wrote a letter, sealed it and tied the letter around the neck of a swan which he loved dearly and concealed it amongst its feathers. He called for a squire and entrusted him with his message. 'Go quickly,' he said, 'change your clothes. You must go to the castle of my beloved and take my swan with you. Mind that you make arrangements, through a servant or maid, that the swan be presented to her.' He did as he was told. Off he went, taking the swan. He followed the straight path which he knew well and arrived at the castle as quickly as possible. He made his way through the town, reached the main gate and called the porter to him. 'Friend,' he said, 'listen to me. I am a man whose trade is such that I am expert at catching birds. In a meadow beneath Caerleon I caught a swan with my net. In order to gain her support and protection, I wish to make a present of it to the lady, to prevent me from being hindered and arraigned in this region.' [153–90] The young man replied: 'Friend, no one speaks with her; but nevertheless I shall see what I can discover. If I could find a spot to which I could take you, I would let you speak to her.' The porter went to the hall, where just two knights were to be found sitting at a large table enjoying a game of chess. He came back quickly and led the squire in such a way that no one noticed him and he was not hindered. He reached the bedroom and called out. A maiden opened the door and they approached the lady and presented the swan to her. She summoned a servant and said to him: 'See that my swan is well looked after and given ample food.' 'My lady,' said the man who brought it, 'you are the only one who should receive it. This is indeed a royal gift: see what a fine and handsome bird it is!' He handed it over to her and she received it fittingly. She stroked its neck and head and felt the letter beneath its feathers. Her blood ran cold, for she realized it was from her beloved. She gave the man some money and told him to go. [191–224]

As soon as the bedroom was empty, she called a serving maid. When they had untied the letter, she broke the seal and discovered at the top the name 'Milun'. She recognized her beloved's name and before she could read any further she wept and kissed the letter countless times. After a while she read what was written, what he had commanded her to do and what sorrow and suffering he had undergone day and night. Now he was entirely at her mercy and she could either kill or cure him. If she could discover a stratagem which would enable him to speak with her, she should inform him by letter and send the swan back to him. She should first look after it well, then allow it to go without food for three days. The letter should be hung round the bird's neck. When she let it go, it would fly back to its original home. Having seen what was written and heeded the contents of the letter, she had the swan taken care of and given plenty to eat and drink. She kept it in her chamber for a month. [225–53] But hear now what happened next. Using her ingenuity she got hold of ink and parchment. She was able to write whatever she pleased, and seal the letter with a ring. Having let the swan go without food, she hung the letter round its neck and released it. The bird was famished and eager for food: swiftly it returned home. In Milun's town and in his dwelling it alighted before him. When he saw it, he was full of joy. In great delight he picked it up by the wings. He called a steward and had it fed. He took the letter from its neck, looked at it from top to bottom and rejoiced at the tokens he discovered and the greetings. Without him she could have no happiness. Now he should send back word of his feelings to her in the same way, making use of the swan. This he will do with all haste. [254–78]

Milun and his beloved maintained this way of life for twenty years. The swan acted as messenger. They had no other intermediary and they starved it before releasing it. Whoever received the swan fed it, of course. They came together on a number of occasions. No one can be so imprisoned or so tightly guarded that he cannot find a way out from time to time.

The lady who had brought up her son dubbed him knight. He had been with her long enough to come of age and was a very fine youth. She gave him the letter and the ring, then told him about his mother and what had happened to his father, saying what a good knight he was, so brave, bold and fierce. There was no one in the entire land of greater fame or valour. When the lady had spoken to him and he had listened carefully, he was delighted by his father's good qualities. He was full of joy at what he had heard. He thought to himself and said: 'A man must have a very low opinion of himself, if, when he has been born of such a famous father, he does not establish greater fame beyond his own region and country.' He had everything he required and did not delay more than one night, taking his leave the next day. The lady admonished him greatly, urged him to do well and gave him plenty of money. [279–318]

He made his way to Southampton and set sail as soon as he could. He arrived at Barfleur and went straight to Brittany, where he spent freely and attended tournaments, becoming acquainted with the wealthy. He never participated in any tournament without being considered the best combatant. He loved the poor knights: he gave them what he won from the rich, retained them, and spent lavishly. He never willingly stayed long in one place and carried off the prize and the success in all those foreign fields. He was courtly and knew how to act with honour. News of his skills and his fame reached his homeland: a young man from their region had gone abroad to seek fame and been so successful because of his prowess, excellence and generosity that those who did not know his name everywhere called him The Peerless One. Milun heard the young man praised and his qualities recounted. He felt sad and bewailed the existence of this worthy knight, because, as long as he himself could travel from place to place, attend tournaments and bear arms, no knight born in his land should be praised or esteemed. [319–50] He made up his mind: he would quickly cross the sea and joust with the knight in order to humiliate him and damage his reputation. Anger would drive him on to fight to see if he could unhorse him and finally he would be dishonoured. Then he himself would go in search of his son who had left the country, but he did not know what had become of him. He informed his beloved, as he wished to have her leave to go. He told her exactly what was on his mind and sent a letter and seal, by means of the swan assuredly. Now she should send back word of her feelings. When she heard what he intended to do, she thanked him and was grateful, since he wished to leave the land to seek their son and to display his own worth. She did not wish to stand in his way. Milun received her message, then made lavish preparations, crossed over to Normandy and made his way as far as Brittany, where he made many acquaintances and keenly sought out tournaments. He frequently entertained lavishly and gave generously. [351–80]

Milun spent the whole of one winter in that area, I believe. He retained many knights, until the time came, around Easter, when people recommenced tournaments, wars and fighting. Everyone gathered at Mont St Michel, Normans, Bretons, Flemish and French. But there were very few Englishmen. Milun arrived early. He was a very fine knight and he asked for the other fine knight. There was no lack of people to tell him from which region he had come. Everyone pointed him out to Milun by his arms and his shield and Milun studied him closely. The tournament began and anyone seeking a joust soon found one. Those who briefly searched the ranks could easily win or lose and encounter an opponent. [381–403] I am anxious to tell you about Milun: he performed very well that day in the joust and was highly esteemed. But the young man of whom I speak was acclaimed above all others. No one could compare with him in tourneying and jousting. Milun saw the way he acted and his skill at spurring on his horse and striking blows. However envious he felt at all this, he found it a most pleasing spectacle. He placed himself in the ranks in opposition to him and they jousted together. Milun struck him so hard that in fact he broke his lance-shaft. But he had not unhorsed him and his opponent struck Milun back so forcibly that he knocked him off his horse. He saw beneath his vizor his beard and hoary white hair and was greatly distressed at the fall. He took the horse by the reins and presented it to him, saying: 'Lord, mount your horse. I am most disturbed and saddened that I have committed such an outrageous act against a man of your age.' Milun jumped up. He was very pleased by what had happened. He recognized the ring on his opponent's finger when he returned his horse to him. He addressed the young man. 'Friend,' he said, 'listen to me! For the love of Almighty God, tell me your father's name. What is your name? Who is your mother? I wish to know the whole truth. I have seen a great deal and travelled far, visiting many lands in search of tournaments and wars. Never has any knight forced me off my horse. You have unhorsed me: I could love you tenderly.' [404–46] The other replied: 'I shall tell you as much as I know about my father. I think he was born in Wales and that his name is Milun. He loved the daughter of a wealthy man and I was conceived in secret, then sent to Northumbria and brought up and educated there. One of my aunts raised me. She kept me with her a long time, gave me a horse and arms, and sent me to this land, where I have been for a long time. My intention is to cross the sea very soon and go to my country. I want to know all about my father and how he behaved towards my mother. I shall show him a gold ring and tokens, so that he will have no wish to disown me. Rather will he love and cherish me.' [447–68] When Milun heard him speak thus, he could listen no more. He quickly leaped forward and seized him by the skirt of his hauberk. 'Oh God,' he said, 'now my life is whole again. In truth, friend, you are my son. It was in search of you that I left my country this year.' When the other heard this, he dismounted and kissed his father tenderly. From the joy on their faces and the words they spoke the onlookers wept for joy and emotion. When the tournament was disbanded Milun departed, very anxious to speak to his son at leisure and to let him know his wishes and intentions. That night they were in the same lodgings. Their joy and pleasure was great and with them were a good many knights. Milun told his son about his love for his mother and how her father had given her to a nobleman from the region and how he had continued to love her and she him wholeheartedly. He also told how the swan became his messenger and took his letters, because he dared not trust anyone. The son replied: 'In truth, father, I shall bring you and my mother together. I shall kill her husband and marry her to you.' [469–502]

Then they ceased talking of such things and next day prepared to depart. They took leave of their friends and returned to their country. They soon crossed the sea, for the wind was favourable and strong. As they made their way, they encountered a servant: he came from Milun's beloved and was intending to cross over to Brittany. She had sent him there, but now his task was shortened. He gave Milun a sealed letter and told him verbally that he should come without delay. Her husband was dead, he must now make haste! When Milun heard the news, it seemed quite wonderful to him. He explained this to his son. There was nothing to hinder or delay them. They travelled until they reached the castle where the lady was. She was delighted by her son who was so valiant and noble. They summoned no kinsmen and without the advice of anyone else their son united them and gave his mother to his father. Thereafter they lived night and day in happiness and tenderness. [503–32]

Our ancestors composed a lay about their love and happiness. I who have set it down in writing have had much pleasure in relating it. [533–6]

℈

CHAITIVEL

I am minded to recall a lay of which I have heard and shall recount what happened, name the city where it was composed and tell you its title. It is generally called *Le Chaitivel* ('The Unhappy One'), but many people call it *Les Quatre Deuls* ('The Four Sorrows'). [1–8]

In the city of Nantes in Brittany there dwelt a lady distinguished by her beauty, education and good breeding. There existed no knight in the region with any merit at all who, having once seen her, would not have fallen in love with her and wooed her. It was not possible for her to love them all, but neither did she wish to repulse them. It would be less dangerous for a man to court every lady in an entire land than for a lady to remove a single besotted lover from her skirts, for he will immediately attempt to strike back. She satisfied the desires of each lover at the behest of good will. Yet, even if a lady has no wish to listen to their pleas, she should not speak insultingly to her suitors: rather should she honour and cherish them, serve them appropriately and be grateful to them. The lady whose story I wish to relate was courted constantly because of her beauty and worth and was the object of their attentions night and day. [9–32]

There lived in Brittany four men whose names I do not know. They were not very old, but were exceedingly handsome, brave and valiant knights, generous, courtly and liberal. They were held in very high esteem and were amongst the region's noblemen. The four of them loved the lady and strove to perform brave deeds. Each man did his utmost to win her and have her love, taking great pains to woo her for himself. Each one of them would have thought himself capable of outdoing the others. The lady, who possessed great intelligence, gave careful thought to which of them was more worthy of her love. They all had such great merit that she was unable to choose the best, yet she did not wish to lose all three in order to retain just one. [33–55] To each she displayed a friendly mien; she gave them love tokens and sent her messengers to them. Each was unaware of the other's success, but no one could distinguish between them in any way. Each one thought he could gain the upper hand by the quality of his service and his entreaties. When knights assembled, each one, if he could, would lead all the rest in performing brave deeds in order to please the lady. They all regarded her as their beloved, wore her love token, a ring, sleeve or pennant, and used her name as a rallying cry. She loved and retained all four, until one year, after Easter, a tournament was proclaimed before the city of Nantes. To meet the four lovers, men came from other regions: French, Norman and Flemish knights, those from Brabant, Boulogne and Anjou and from the immediate neighbourhood. They were all glad to come and had been lodged there a good while. [56–82] On the eve of the tournament fierce fighting broke out. The four lovers left the city, fully armed: their knights followed them, but the main burden of the combat rested on these four. Their opponents, recognizing them by their ensigns and shields, sent knights to oppose them, two from Flanders and two from Hainault, ready and equipped for combat. To a man they were keen to join battle. The lovers saw them approach, but had no thoughts of flight. Lance lowered and at full speed, each one picked out his opponent. The blows were so vehement that the four adversaries were unhorsed. The lovers did not trouble to seize the horses, but left them riderless. They took up position against the fallen combatants whose knights came to their aid; a great mêlée ensued as their men tried to rescue them and swords struck many a blow. From a tower the lady could see clearly her knights and their men. She witnessed her lovers giving a good account of themselves and did not know which merited her esteem the most. [83–110]

The tournament began. The ranks increased and swelled and many battles were joined that day before the city gates. Her four lovers performed so well that by nightfall, when it was time to leave the field, they had carried off all the honours. Very foolishly they strayed far from their followers and for this they paid the price. For three of them were killed and the fourth was injured and wounded in the thigh in such a way that the lance passed right through his body. They were hit by a lateral attack and all four were unhorsed. Those who had mortally wounded them threw their shields to the ground, grief-stricken on their account, as they had not intended to kill them. A great outcry and clamour arose; such sorrow had never before been heard. The inhabitants of the city came out on to the field with no fear of the other fighters. In their grief over the knights a full two thousand men unfastened their visors and tore at their hair and beards, united in their sorrow. Each knight was placed on his shield and carried into the city to the lady who had loved them. [111–42] As soon as she discovered what had happened, she fell to the ground in a swoon. When she revived, she lamented each one by name. 'Alas,' she said, 'whatever shall I do? I shall never again be happy! I loved these four knights and desired each one for his own sake. There was a great deal of good in them all and they loved me above everything. Because they were so handsome, brave, worthy and generous, I made them compete for my love, not wishing to lose them all to have just one. I do not know which of them to mourn the most, but I can no longer disguise or hide my feelings. One of them I now see wounded and three are dead. There remains no comfort for me in this world, so I shall bury the dead, and if the injured knight can be healed, I shall gladly take care of him and provide him with a good doctor.' She had him carried into her chamber and then arranged for the others to be laid out for burial, lovingly, nobly and lavishly arrayed. She gave a large offering and substantial gift to a rich abbey where they were buried. May God have mercy on them! She had summoned learned doctors and the knight lying wounded in her chamber was placed in their charge until he was cured. She visited him often and comforted him very well. But she mourned the others and was grief-stricken at what had befallen them. [143–80]

One summer's day, after dinner, the lady was conversing with the knight. She was reminded of her great sorrow and deep in thought bowed her face and head. He looked at her, realizing she was lost in thought, and spoke kindly to her: 'My lady, you are in distress. What are you thinking about? Tell me. Put aside your grief and be comforted.' 'My friend,' she replied, 'I was thinking, and recalling your companions. Never will a lady of my lineage, however beautiful, worthy or wise, love four such men at once and in a single day lose them all, except for you alone who were wounded. You came dangerously close to death, so because of my great love for you all, I want my grief to be remembered. I shall compose a lay about the four of you and entitle it *The Four Sorrows*.' [181–204] When he heard these words, the knight replied quickly: 'My lady, compose the new lay, but call it *The Unhappy One*. I shall explain why it should have this title. The others have long since ended their days and used up their span of life. What great anguish they suffered on account of the love they bore for you! But I who have escaped alive, bewildered and forlorn, constantly see the woman I love more than anything on earth, coming and going; she speaks to me morning and evening, yet I cannot experience the joy of a kiss or an embrace or of any pleasure other than conversation. You cause me to suffer a hundred such ills and death would be preferable for me. Therefore the lay will be named after me and called *The Unhappy One*. Anyone who calls it *The Four Sorrows* will be changing its true name.' 'Upon my word,' she replied, 'I am agreeable to this: let us now call it *The Unhappy One*.' [205–30]

Thus was the lay begun, and later completed and performed. Some of those who put it into circulation call it *The Four Sorrows*. Each name is appropriate and supported by the subject matter. It is commonly known as *The Unhappy One*. Here it ends, for there is no more. I have heard no more, know no more and shall relate no more to you. [231–40]

XI

CHEVREFOIL

It pleases me greatly and I am eager to relate to you the truth of the lay called *Chevrefoil*, to say why it was composed and how it originated. Many people have recited it to me and I have also found it in a written form. It concerns Tristram and the queen: their love was so pure that it caused them to suffer great distress and later brought about their death on the same day. [1-10]

King Mark was angry with his nephew Tristram and he dismissed him from his land because of his love for the queen. Tristram made his way to his own region and could not return. He spent a whole year in South Wales, where he was born. But then he ran the risk of death and destruction. Do not in any way be surprised; for anyone who loves with great loyalty is severely distressed and forlorn, if he cannot satisfy his desires. Tristram was distressed and downcast and for this reason left his own land and made his way straight to Cornwall where the queen lived. To avoid being seen he took to the forest all alone, only emerging in the evening when it was time to take shelter. At night he took lodging with peasants and poor people and asked them for news of the king's activities. They told him they had heard that a proclamation had been issued summoning the barons to Tintagel. The king wished to hold court there and everyone would be present at Pentecost. There would be much merrymaking and rejoicing and the queen would be with them. [11-43]

Tristram received this news with great joy, for she would not be able to travel there without his seeing her pass by. On the day the king set out, Tristram entered the wood along the road he knew the procession would have to take. He cut a hazel branch in half and squared it. When he had whittled the stick he wrote his name on it with his knife. If the queen, who would be on the look-out, spotted it (on an earlier occasion she had successfully observed it in this way), she would recognize her beloved's stick when she saw it.

That was all he wrote, because he had sent her word that he had been there a long time, waiting patiently and watching out for an opportunity to see her, for he could not possibly live without her.[1] The two of them resembled the honeysuckle which clings to the hazel branch: when it has wound itself round and attached itself to the hazel, the two can survive together: but if anyone should then attempt to separate them, the hazel quickly dies, as does the honeysuckle. 'Sweet love, so it is with us: without me you cannot survive, nor I without you. [44–78]

The queen rode along. She looked at the path as it sloped upwards ahead of her, saw the piece of wood and realized what it was. She recognized all the letters and commanded all those who were escorting her and travelling along with her to stop. She wished to alight and take a rest. They did as she bade and she moved a good distance away from her companions, calling her faithful servant Brenguein to her. She went a little way off the path and in the wood she found the man who loved her more than any living thing. They shared great joy together. He spoke freely to her and she told him of her desires. Then she explained how he could be reconciled with the king and how disturbed the king had been at having to banish him. He had done it because of the accusation against him. Then she departed, leaving her beloved behind. But, when the moment came for them to separate, they began to weep. Tristram returned to Wales until his uncle summoned him. [79–106]

On account of the joy he had experienced from the sight of his beloved and because of what he had written, Tristram, a skilful harpist, in order to record his words (as the queen had said he should), used them to create a new lay. I shall very briefly name it: the English call it *Gotelef* and the French *Chevrefoil*. I have told you the truth of the lay I have related here. [107–18]

XII

ELIDUC

I shall tell you the story and the whole substance of a very old Breton lay, in so far as I understand the truth of it. [1–4]

In Brittany there was a knight, worthy and courtly, brave and fierce: Eliduc was his name, I believe, and there was no man so valiant in the land. His wife was noble and wise, of good family and high-born. They lived together for a long time and loved each other with great loyalty, but then it happened that he went in search of paid military service. There he loved a maiden, the daughter of a king and queen, whose name was Guilliadun, and none in the kingdom was more beautiful. His wife, whose name was Guildelüec, remained in her country. From these two the lay of *Guildelüec and Guilliadun* takes its name. It was first called *Eliduc*, but now the name has been changed, because the adventure upon which the lay is based concerns the ladies. I shall relate to you the truth of it as it happened. [5–28]

Eliduc's lord, the King of Brittany, loved him dearly and cherished him. He served the king loyally and, whenever the king was away, the land was Eliduc's to guard. The king retained Eliduc for his prowess and as a result many advantages accrued to him. He could hunt in the forest and no forester was bold enough to oppose him or even grumble at him in any way. The envy of his good fortune, which often possesses others, caused him to be embroiled with his lord, to be slandered and accused, so that he was banished from the court without a formal accusation. Eliduc did not know why and often beseeched the king to hear his defence and not to believe slander, for he had served him long and willingly. But the king did not answer him and, since his lord refused to listen, he was obliged to depart. He returned to his house, summoned all his friends and told them of the anger which his lord, the king, felt towards him. He had served him to the best of his ability and ought not to have deserved his ill-will. [29–60] The rustics say in a proverb that when he admonishes his ploughman a lord's love is no fief. He who is loyal to his lord and loves his good neighbours is wise and sensible. Eliduc did not want to stay in the country and said that he would cross the sea to the kingdom of Logres to take his ease for a while. He would leave his wife at home and order his men to look after her faithfully, and all his friends likewise. He kept this counsel and equipped himself richly. His friends were very sad that he was leaving them. He took only ten knights with him, and his wife, who bewailed her husband's departure, escorted him at his leaving, but he assured her that he would keep good faith with her. Thereupon he parted from her and pursued his path onwards. Coming to the sea, he crossed it and arrived at Totnes. [61–88]

There were a number of kings in that land and there was great strife and war between them. In this country, near Exeter, lived a very old and powerful man, who had no male heir of his own, just a daughter of marriageable age. Because he refused to give her to one of his peers, this latter was making war upon him and laying waste all his lands. The enemy had surrounded him in a castle where no man was bold enough to resist and engage in single combat or in mêlée, but when Eliduc heard of this he would proceed no further now that he had found a war. He wanted to remain in that country to help as best he could the king who was most afflicted and discomfited, and remain in his service. He sent messengers and informed the king in a letter that he had left his own country and come to his aid, asking him to make known his wishes and, if he did not want to retain him, to grant him safe conduct through the land. He would then go further in search of service. [89–118] When the king saw the messengers, he received them eagerly and honourably. He called his constable and quickly ordered him to prepare an escort to bring the baron there, to prepare hostels where they could lodge and to give them as much as they would need for a month's expenditure. The escort was prepared and sent to fetch Eliduc, who was received with great honour and made very welcome by the king. His lodging was with a very wise and courtly burgess, who turned over to him his fine chamber hung with curtains. Eliduc ensured that he was well-served and had all the poor knights who were lodged in the town come to his table.

He forbade all his men to be so bold as to accept any gift or money during the first forty days. [119–44]

On the third day of their stay the cry went up in the city that their enemies had come and were spread throughout the land, intending to assault the town and come right up to the gates. Eliduc heard the tumult of the frightened people and armed himself without delay, as did his companions. There were forty mounted knights staying in the town – a number were wounded and there were many prisoners – and when they saw Eliduc mount they went to their lodgings to arm themselves. They left with him by the gate, not waiting to be summoned. 'Lord,' they said, 'we shall go with you and do as you do!' He replied: 'I thank you. Does anyone know of a narrow pass or defile where we can ambush the enemy? If we await them here, we could join battle with them, but this would not be to our advantage if anyone knows a better plan.' They said to him: 'Lord, truly, near this wood, in a thicket, is a narrow cart-track along which they must return. When they have captured their spoils, they will return thence. They often come back unarmed on their palfreys, thus openly courting death. It would be easy to inflict losses on them, humiliate them and make them suffer.' [145–84] Eliduc said to them: 'Friends, I pledge my faith to you in this matter: he who does not sometimes go where he surely thinks he will lose will gain little and never rise in esteem. You are all vassals of the king and should thus remain loyal to him, so come with me wherever I go and do as I do. I promise you faithfully that you will meet no obstacle as long as I can help it, and, if we can win anything, the discomfiting of our enemies will increase our reputation.' They accepted his pledge and took him to the wood, hiding in the bushes near the path until the enemy returned. Eliduc showed them exactly how to engage the enemy and how to shout at them. When the enemy had entered the pass, Eliduc shouted after them and called to all his companions, exhorting them to do well. They struck vigorously and did not spare the enemy, who were quite astounded, quickly routed and their ranks split, being vanquished in a short time. [185–217] Their constable and many other knights were held and entrusted to the keeping of the squires. Twenty-five men on Eliduc's side captured thirty of the enemy. They quickly seized the equipment, took much booty and then returned joyfully, having achieved much. The king was in a tower, much afraid for his men, and lamented Eliduc loudly for he thought and feared that he had abandoned his knights. But they arrived back in a body, loaded with booty, their number greater upon their return than it had been when they left; because of this, the king failed to recognize them and harboured doubts and suspicions. He ordered the gates shut and told his people to climb on to the walls to shoot at them and bombard them. They would have no need of this, however, for the party had sent in advance a squire on a swift steed, who related the adventure to them, told them of the soldier, how he had defeated the enemy and how he had conducted himself. There was never such a knight, they said. [218–49] He had taken the constable, captured twenty-nine of the others, and killed and wounded many more. When the king heard the news, he was exceedingly joyful and came down from the tower to meet Eliduc. He thanked him for his kindness and Eliduc surrendered the prisoners to him, distributing the arms to the others and keeping for his own use only three horses, which were highly praised. He shared and gave away everything, including his own portion, to both the prisoners and the others.

After this deed I have related to you, the king loved and cherished Eliduc greatly, retaining him for a whole year along with his companions. He received his allegiance and made him custodian of his land. [250–70]

Eliduc was courtly and wise, a fine knight, worthy and generous, and the king's daughter heard tell of him and his virtues. She sent her personal chamberlain to him to request and summon him to come and relax for a while with her, so that they might talk and become acquainted. She was most surprised that he had not come to her, but Eliduc replied that he would go and make her acquaintance willingly. He mounted his steed, taking a knight with him, and then went to talk to the maiden. Before he entered the chamber he sent the chamberlain on ahead and delayed a little until the latter returned. With gentle mien, honest expression and very noble demeanour, he spoke with much breeding and thanked the damsel, Guilliadun, who was very beautiful, for having sent for him to come and talk to her. She took him by the hand and they sat down on a bed and spoke of many things. [271–99] She looked at him closely, at his face, his body and his appearance, saying to herself that there was nothing unbecoming about him and forming a great admiration for him. Love dispatched its messenger who summoned her to love him. It made her go pale and sigh, but she did not want to discuss the matter with him lest he blame her for it. He stayed there a long while, then took his leave and left. She granted him leave very unwillingly, but he nevertheless departed and returned to his lodging. He was very sad and pensive, and anxious because this beautiful girl, the daughter of his lord the king, had addressed him so gently and sighed. He considered himself most unfortunate to have been in the country for so long and to have seen her so little. Having said this, he repented of it, for he remembered his wife, and how he had assured her that he would be faithful and behave loyally. [300–326]

When she had seen him, the maiden wanted him for her lover. She had never esteemed anyone as much and wanted to keep him with her if she could. Thus she stayed awake the whole night and neither rested nor slept. She arose the next morning, went to a window, calling her chamberlain in whom she confided fully. 'By my faith,' she said, 'how unfortunate I am! I have fallen into a sorry plight, for I love the new soldier, Eliduc, the good knight. I had no rest last night and could not close my eyes to sleep. If he wishes to love me truly and will pledge himself to me, I shall do whatever he wants; he could benefit greatly from it and be king of this land. He is so exceedingly wise and courtly that, if he does not love me truly, I shall have to die a mournful death.' When she had spoken thus, the chamberlain whom she had summoned gave her some loyal advice with which he should not be reproached. 'Lady,' he said, 'if you love him, send someone to ask him to come and send him a girdle, a ribbon or ring, for this will please him. If he receives it gladly and is happy about the summons, then you will be sure of his love. There is no emperor on earth who ought not to be glad if you wanted to love him.' [327–64] When she had heard his advice, the maiden replied: 'How shall I know from my present whether he is inclined to love me? I have never seen a knight who received such a request, whether he felt love or hate, who did not willingly keep any present sent to him. I should hate him to mock me. But we may nevertheless learn something of the man from his mien. Get yourself ready and go.' 'I am ready now,' he replied. 'You will take him a gold ring and give him my girdle. Greet him a thousand times on my behalf.' The chamberlain departed and she remained thus. Although she almost called him back, she nevertheless let him go and began to lament: 'Alas, how my heart has been taken unawares by a man from another country! I do not even know if he is of a noble family. He will soon leave and I shall be left behind to mourn, for I was foolish to set my mind on this. I only spoke of it yesterday and now already I am begging him for his love. I think he may blame me, but if he is courtly, he will be grateful. Now the die is cast and, if he does not care for my love, I shall consider myself unfortunate and shall have no joy for the rest of my life.' [365–400]

While she was lamenting, the chamberlain hurried to Eliduc and greeted him secretly, telling him the maiden had asked to see him. He presented Eliduc with the ring and the girdle and the knight thanked him, put the golden ring on his finger and the girdle around him. The young man said no more, nor did Eliduc inquire further, but only offered him a present of his own. He left, refusing to take anything. He returned to his lady and found her in her chamber, and when he had greeted her on Eliduc's behalf and thanked her for the gift, she said: 'Come now, hide nothing from me! Does he want to love me truly?' He replied: 'This is my opinion: the knight is not fickle. I consider him courtly and wise, and he knows well how to conceal his feelings. I greeted him on your behalf and gave him your gifts. He put on your girdle, attaching it securely around his waist and put the ring on his finger. I said nothing more to him, nor he to me.' [401–30] 'Did he not receive it as a love-token? If not, then I am betrayed.' He replied: 'By my faith, I do not know, but listen to what I am about to tell you: if he did not wish you well, then he would want nothing of yours.' 'You jest,' she said. 'I know he does not hate me, for I never did him any harm, except by loving him so deeply. If he still wants to hate me, he deserves to die. I shall never ask anything else of him through you or anyone else until I speak to him. I want to show him myself how my love for him afflicts me, but I do not know if he will stay.' The chamberlain replied: 'Lady, the king has retained him on oath for a year to serve him faithfully. Thus you will have enough opportunity to show him your desire.' When she heard he would be remaining, she rejoiced greatly, very glad he was staying. She knew nothing of the sadness he had felt since seeing her, but he had no joy or pleasure, except when thinking of her. [431–61] He considered himself unfortunate, for he had promised his wife, before leaving his own country, that he would love only her. Now his heart was firmly trapped, for he wanted to remain faithful, but could not refrain from loving the maiden Guilliadun, who was so beautiful, from looking at her and talking to her, kissing and embracing her. However, he would never ask her for her love, which would redound to his dishonour, both in order to keep faith with his wife, and because he was in the king's service. In great distress, Eliduc mounted up and delayed no longer, calling his companions to him. He went to the castle to talk to the king and wanted to see the maiden if he could, as she was the reason why he had set out. The king rose from the table, went into his daughter's rooms and began to play chess with a knight from over the sea, who sat at the other side of the chessboard and whose duty it was to teach his daughter. Eliduc approached, and the king welcomed him warmly, making him sit down beside him. [462–91] He then called his daughter and said to her: 'Damsel, you should become well acquainted with this knight and show him great honour. There is none better in five hundred.' When the girl had listened to what her lord had commanded, she was very glad, and she arose and spoke to Eliduc. They sat well apart from the others, both caught in love's grip, but she dared not address him and he was fearful about talking to her, apart from thanking her for the present she had sent him: he had never cherished any possession more. She answered the knight that she was glad of this and that she had sent him the ring, and the girdle as well, because she had granted him possession of herself. She loved him so much and wanted to make him her husband and, if she could not have him, he truly ought to know that she would have no man alive. Now, she said, he ought to tell her his wishes. [492–518] 'Lady,' he replied, 'I am very grateful to you for your love and it gives me much joy. Since you esteem me so much, I ought to be very glad of this and will not forget it. I have agreed to remain one year with the king who took my oath that I would not leave until his war was over. Then I shall return to my country, as I wish to remain no longer, providing you will give me leave.' The maiden answered him: 'Beloved, I thank you profusely! You are so wise and courtly that before then you will have decided what to do about me. I love and trust you above anything else.' They pledged each other their troth and spoke no more on that occasion. Eliduc went to his lodgings and was very happy, for he had achieved much. He could often speak with his beloved and great was the love between them. His efforts in the war were so successful that he captured and retained the king's adversary, and freed the whole land. He was greatly valued for his prowess, his wisdom and his generosity. Good fortune had befallen him. [519–49]

While all this was taking place, his own lord had sent out three messengers to look for him, to say that he was being set upon and injured. He was losing all his castles and all his land was being laid waste. He had often regretted that Eliduc had left him and had been ill-advised to view him with disfavour. He had cast out of the country and exiled for ever those traitors who had accused Eliduc, who had blamed him and caused him to be embroiled with his lord. In his dire need he summoned and required Eliduc by the promise he had made when he had accepted his homage to come and help him, for he stood in great need. [550–70]

Eliduc heard the news and was much disturbed for the maiden's sake, for he loved her dearly and she him as much as possible. There was no foolishness between them, nor fickleness, nor wickedness, as their love consisted entirely of courting and talking, and exchanging fair gifts when they were together. It was her intention and her hope to make him hers completely and keep him if she could, but she did not know that he had a wife. 'Alas,' he said, 'I have behaved badly! I have been too long in this country. Alas that ever I saw it! Here I have deeply loved a girl, Guilliadun, the king's daughter, and she has loved me. If I must leave her thus, one of us will have to die, or perhaps even both. But nevertheless I must go, for my lord has summoned me in a letter and required me by my oath, and my wife as well. Now I must take care. I can remain no longer and must leave. If I were to marry my beloved, the Christian religion would not accept it. Things are going badly in all respects. God, parting is so hard! But whoever may blame me for it, I shall always do right by my beloved. I shall do as she wishes and act according to her advice. The king, her lord, is now at peace and henceforth I think no one will make war upon him. In my own lord's interests I shall seek to depart before the day set to mark the end of my stay here with the king. I shall go and talk with the maiden and inform her fully about my situation. She will tell me her wishes and I shall carry them out as best I can.' [571–618]

The knight delayed no more and went to take leave of the king. He told him what had happened and read him the letter sent by his lord, who was summoning him in great distress. When the king heard the summons, he realized Eliduc would not remain and was very sad and disturbed. He offered him a large share of his possessions and surrendered to him his treasure and a third of his heritage. He would do so much to make him stay that Eliduc would thereafter always be grateful to him. 'God,' he said, 'since my lord is in distress and has summoned me from such a distance, this time I shall go to his aid; nothing would keep me here. If you need my service, I shall willingly return to you with a great force of knights.' The king thanked him for this and gladly gave him leave, putting all the wealth of his house at his disposal, gold and silver, dogs and horses, and silken clothes, fine and fair. Eliduc took a moderate quantity and then, as was fitting, said he would go and speak with his daughter, if he agreed. The king replied: 'That would please me.' [619–51] The king sent ahead a squire to open the chamber door. Eliduc went to talk with her and when she saw him she spoke to him and greeted him six thousand times. He consulted her about the matter and briefly explained to her his journey, but before he had told her everything, or begged or taken his leave, she fainted with grief and lost all her colour. When Eliduc saw her faint he began to moan and kissed her mouth often and wept most tenderly. He took her and held her in his arms until she recovered from her swoon. 'Ah God,' he said, 'sweet love, let me tell you something: you are my life and my death, in you is all my comfort! I consulted you because of the pledge between us, but of necessity I must go to my country. I have taken leave of your father, but I shall do what you wish, whatever may befall me.' 'Take me away with you,' she said, 'since you will remain no longer! If not, I shall kill myself and never have joy or happiness again.' Eliduc replied gently that he loved her deeply and truly: 'Fair one, in truth I belong by an oath to your father up to the appointed time – if I were to take you away with me, I should betray my faith. Loyally I swear and pledge to you that, if you give me leave, grant me a postponement and set a day by which you wish me to return, nothing on earth will keep me from doing so, providing I am alive and well. My life is completely in your hands.' She had great love for him and so set a period and fixed the day on which he was to return and take her away. They grieved much on parting, exchanged their golden rings and kissed each other affectionately. [652–702]

He came to the sea, where the wind was good, and soon crossed. When Eliduc had arrived, his lord was joyful and glad, as were his friends, relations and everyone else, above all his good wife, who was very beautiful, wise and worthy. But he was still distracted by the love that had taken him unawares, and he displayed no joyful or friendly mien, whatever he saw, nor would he indeed be joyful until he saw his beloved. He behaved most secretively and his wife was sad in her heart because of this, not knowing what it meant. She lamented to herself and often asked him whether someone had told him that she had misbehaved or done wrong while he had been out of the country, for she would willingly defend herself in front of his people, if he wished. [703–26] 'Lady,' he said, 'I do not accuse you of any crime or misdemeanour, but in the country where I have been I pledged and swore to the king that I should return to him; now he has great need of me. If my lord the king were at peace, I should not stay another week. Great torment will come my way before I can return, and nothing will make me happy until I have done so, for I do not want to break my word.' At this the lady let the matter rest. Eliduc was with his lord, whom he aided greatly. The king acted on his advice and took steps to safeguard the whole land, but when the time approached which the maiden had appointed, Eliduc strove to make peace. He reconciled the king with all his enemies, and then prepared himself for departure together with those he wished to take with him. He took only two of his nephews whom he loved, a chamberlain of his (who had been privy to their plans and had borne the message) and his squires, for he wanted no others. He made these pledge and swear to keep his affair secret. [727–58]

Waiting no longer, he put to sea and they were soon on the other side. He arrived in the region where he was greatly desired, but Eliduc was very sensible and took lodging far from the harbour, for he did not want to be seen, discovered or recognized. He prepared his chamberlain and sent him to his beloved to inform her of his arrival and that he had kept his covenant. That night, when all was dark, she was to leave the city; the chamberlain would go with her and Eliduc himself would come to meet her. The chamberlain had changed all his garments and went swiftly on foot to the city where the king's daughter was. He sought and inquired until he found his way into her chamber, where he greeted the damsel and said that her beloved had come. Whereas she had been mournful and dismayed before, when she heard the news she wept tenderly for joy and kissed the chamberlain several times. He told her that she would have to leave with him at nightfall and thus they remained the whole day, planning their route well. At night, when all was dark, she and the young man left the town, the two of them alone, but she was still frightened lest anyone see her. She was dressed in a silken garment finely embroidered with gold, with a short cloak attached. [759–98]

A bow's shot from the gate was a wood surrounded by a beautiful pasture. Her beloved, who had come on her account, waited for them at the foot of the palissade, towards which the chamberlain led her. Eliduc dismounted and kissed her and they were most joyful at their reunion. He made her mount a horse and then mounted himself, taking the reins. He quickly departed with her and came to the harbour at Totnes, where they boarded the ship straightaway. There was no one on board, save his own men and his beloved Guilliadun. They had a good wind and settled weather, but as they were about to arrive, they encountered a storm at sea and a wind arose before them that drove them far from the harbour. Their mast broke and split and the sail was completely torn. They solemnly called upon God, St Nicholas and St Clement, and upon the Virgin Mary to beseech her son to help them and save them from destruction and so enable them to reach the harbour. They sailed back and forth along the coast and came extremely close to being shipwrecked. [799–829] Then one of the sailors cried aloud: 'What are we doing? Lord, you have with you the woman who will cause us to perish. We shall never make land! You have a loyal wife and now with this other woman you offend God and his law, righteousness and the faith. Let us cast her into the sea and we shall soon arrive safely.' Eliduc heard what he said and almost went demented with anger. 'Son of a whore,' he said, 'wicked and evil traitor, say no more! If I had abandoned my love, you would have paid dearly for it.' But he held her in his arms and comforted her as best he could against her sea-sickness and because she had heard that he had a wife in his own country. She fell face down, quite pale and wan, in a swoon in which she remained, for she did not come round or breathe. He who was taking her away with him truly believed that she was dead. [830–58] He lamented greatly and then arose, went quickly up to the sailor and struck him with the oar so that he knocked him out flat. Then with his foot he pushed him overboard and the waves bore the body away. When he had cast him into the sea, he went to take charge of the helm, steering the boat and holding it on course so that he reached the harbour and land. When they had arrived, he put down the gangway and dropped anchor. Guilliadun still lay in a swoon, seemingly dead, and Eliduc lamented loudly, for he would gladly have died with her. He asked each of his companions for advice on where he could bear the maiden, for he would not leave her. She would be interred and buried with great honour and with a fine service in a consecrated cemetery, for she was a king's daughter and had a right to this. They were quite forlorn, unable to give him any advice, and so Eliduc began to think where he could take her. His dwelling was close to the sea and he could be there by dinner time. All around it was a forest, thirty leagues in circumference, where a holy hermit, who had been there for forty years, lived and had a chapel. Eliduc had spoken with him many times. He decided to take her to him and have her buried in his chapel. He would provide a large portion of his land to found an abbey there and establish a convent of monks, nuns or canons who would always pray for her. May God be merciful to her! He had his horses brought and ordered his companions to mount, making them swear that they would not betray him. He carried his beloved before him on his palfrey. [859–908]

They rode straight onwards until they entered the wood and came to the chapel, where they called and knocked, but found no one to answer them or to open the door, so Eliduc sent one of his men inside to unlock and open it. Eight days earlier, the holy, saintly hermit had passed away, and when Eliduc found the newly dug tomb, he was most aggrieved and upset. The others wanted to dig the grave where he was to place his beloved, but he made them draw back and said to them: 'This is not correct, for I shall first take counsel with the wise men of the country about how I can glorify the place either as an abbey or as a church. We shall lay her before the altar and commend her to God.' He had sheets brought and they made a bed for her at once, laying the girl on it and leaving her for dead. But when it came to parting, he thought he would die of grief, and he kissed her eyes and her face, saying: 'Fair one, may it never please God for me to bear arms again or live and endure in this world! Fair love, how sad that you ever laid eyes on me! Sweet darling, how sad that you followed me! Fair one, you would soon have been a queen, but for the loyal and pure love with which you loved me so faithfully. My heart grieves because of you and the day I bury you I shall take holy orders. On your tomb every day I shall make my grief resound.' Then he left the maiden and closed the chapel door. [909–952]

He had sent a messenger home to tell his wife that he was coming, but that he was weary and upset. When she heard this, she was very glad and prepared to meet him. She received her lord properly, but little joy awaited her, for he showed no friendly mien nor spoke fair words, and no one dared address him. He was in the house for two days and then heard mass in the morning and set off. He went to the chapel in the woods where the damsel lay and found her still in a swoon, for she neither recovered nor even breathed. It seemed astonishing to him to see the colour in her cheeks still, for she had lost little of it and was only a trifle paler. He wept in anguish and prayed for her soul. When he had finished his prayer, he returned to his house. [953–78]

One day his wife had one of her servants spy on Eliduc as he left the church. She promised him a large reward if he followed at a distance and took note of which direction her lord took. If he did this, she would give him horse and arms. He obeyed her command, taking to the woods and following Eliduc without being noticed. He saw how he entered the chapel and heard the lamentation he made, but before Eliduc came out he had returned to his lady, telling all he had heard, the lamentation, the noise, and the cries that her husband had made in the hermitage. She was disturbed by this and said: 'We shall go straightaway and search the hermitage thoroughly. My husband has to go out, I think, for he is going to court to talk to the king. The hermit died some time ago, and even though I know that my husband loved him well, he would not do this on his account, nor show much grief.' Such was her conclusion on this occasion. [979–1005]

On the afternoon of the same day, when Eliduc went to talk to the king, the lady took the servant with her and he led her to the hermitage. When she entered the chapel and saw the bed of the maiden who was like a new rose, she raised the coverlet and saw the body so slender, the long arms, the white hands, the fingers, slim, long, and full. Then she knew why her husband had grieved. She called the servant and showed him the marvel: 'Do you see this woman,' she said, 'who in beauty resembles a gem? This is my husband's beloved for whom he laments so, and, in faith, it is no wonder when such a beautiful woman has perished. Either pity or love will prevent me from ever knowing joy again.' She began to weep and lament the damsel and, as she sat weeping in front of the bed, a weasel, which had come out from beneath the altar, ran past, and the servant struck it because it passed over the body. He killed it with a stick and threw it on the floor. [1006–37] It did not take long for another to run up which, seeing the first one lying there, walked around its head, touching it often with its foot. Unable to rouse its partner, it seemed distressed and left the chapel, going into the woods in search of herbs. With its teeth the weasel picked a flower, bright red in colour, and then quickly returned, placing it in the mouth of its companion, whom the servant had killed, with the result that it quickly recovered. The lady noticed this and shouted to the servant: 'Catch it! Throw your stick, good man, do not let it escape!' And he threw it and hit the weasel so that the flower fell from its mouth. The lady arose, picked it up and quickly came back, placing the beautiful flower inside the maiden's mouth.[1] After a short while she revived and breathed. Then she spoke and opened her eyes: 'God,' she said, 'I have slept so long!' [1038–66] When the lady heard her speak, she began to thank God and asked her who she was. The girl said: 'Lady, I was born in Logres, the daughter of a king of that country. I deeply loved a knight, Eliduc, the good soldier, who took me away with him. He sinned when he tricked me, for he has a wife and never told me or even gave any indication of this, and so, when I heard about his wife, my grief caused me to faint. He has wickedly left me forlorn in another land and has betrayed me. I do not know what to think. She who trusts a man is extremely foolish.' 'Fair one,' the lady replied, 'nothing on earth could make him joyful, you may be assured of that, for he thinks you are dead and is terribly distressed. He has come to look at you every day, but I assume he found you in a swoon. Truly, I am his wife and my heart grieves for him. Because of the grief he displayed, I wanted to know where he went, and came after him and found you. I am overjoyed that you are alive and shall take you with me and return you to your beloved. I shall set him free completely and take the veil.' The lady comforted the girl until she was able to take her away with her. [1067–104]

She made her servant ready and sent him for her husband. He searched until he found him and then greeted him courteously, telling him the story. Eliduc mounted on a horse, but did not wait for his companions and returned that night to his house. When he found his beloved alive, he thanked his wife gently. Eliduc was extremely happy, and had never been so joyful. He often kissed the maiden and she him tenderly, for together they were very happy. When the lady saw how they looked, she spoke to her husband and asked him for permission to leave and to separate from him, for she wanted to be a nun and serve God. He could give her some of his land, on which she could found an abbey, and then marry the girl he loved so much, for it was neither right nor proper to keep two wives, nor should the law allow it. Eliduc granted his wife this and willingly gave her leave, for he would do everything she wanted and give her some land. Near the castle in the woods, where the hermitage chapel stood, she had her church and houses built. It was endowed with much land and great possessions and would have everything it needed. When everything had been properly prepared, she took the veil, as did thirty nuns with her. Then she established her way of life and the rules of her order. [1105–44]

Eliduc married his beloved. On the wedding day the celebrations were conducted with great honour and a fine service. They lived together for many a day and the love between them was perfect. They distributed great alms and great wealth until such time as they themselves turned to God. Near the castle, on the other side, Eliduc wisely and carefully built a church, which he endowed with most of his land and all his gold and silver. There he placed his own men and other pious persons to uphold the order and maintain the house. When everything was ready, he hardly delayed, but joined himself to them in order to serve almighty God. He placed his dear wife together with his first one and the latter received her as her sister and showed her great honour, urging her to serve God and teaching her the order. They prayed that God might show their beloved His sweet mercy and Eliduc in turn prayed for them, sending his messenger to see how they fared and how their spirits were. Each one strove to love God in good faith and they came to a good end thanks to God, the true divine. [1145–80]

From the story of these three the ancient courtly Bretons composed a lay to be remembered, so that it should not be forgotten. [1181–4]

NOTES

GUIGEMAR

1. The rote was a harp of five strings, rather like a zither.

YONEC

1. The lady's husband is designated in Marie's text as an *avouez* (v. 13). It is possible that this term is a general one describing the lord of the city, the holder of the fief. But it is more likely that Marie is referring to the official functions of the advocate (*advocatus*), the officer appointed by the Church to handle its secular affairs. The advocates seem often to have usurped the land they were supposed to protect and to have set themselves up as independent feudal lords. The distaste felt by many for the advocate would emphasize the plight of the lady, married off to him in order to produce an heir to lands which should rightfully revert on his death to the Church.

CHEVREFOIL

1. Lines 60–61 read, with Ewert's punctuation, '*Ceo fu la summe de l'escrit / Qu'il li avoit mandé e dit:*'. These lines are usually rendered as 'This was the gist of the message which he had sent her'. The present interpretation is based on a change in punctuation: '*Ceo fu la summe do l'escrit. / Qu'il li aveit mandé e dit / Que lunges ot ilec esté . . .*'. See G. S. Burgess, *The Lais of Marie de France: Text and Context*, Chapter 4.

ELIDUC

1. The gender of the weasels is difficult to determine. The Old French *musteile* is feminine, as is the Modern French *belette*. It is tempting to see the pair as a male and a female, but in this case the translation of R. Hanning and J. Ferrante, in which the first weasel appears as a female and the second as a male, can be compared with that of E. Mason, for whom a female resuscitates a male. However, it could well be that we should take both weasels to be female. In his study 'The Weasel in Religion, Myth and Superstition' (*Washington University Studies*, 12, 1924, 33–66) T. S. Duncan points out that the weasel 'may have been generally thought of as a female animal' (p. 44) and that in cases of metamorphosis 'the weasel is always transformed into a woman and never into a man' (ibid.). In this case the weasels could be envisaged as a reflection of Eliduc's two ladies. In folklore the weasel is credited with knowledge of the herb of life. The red flower, which could be the verbena, is probably symbolic of the flow of blood and the restoration of life to the dead girl.

BIBLIOGRAPHY

For a more complete list of titles consult G. S. Burgess, *Marie de France: an Analytical Bibliography* (London: Grant and Cutler, 1977; Supplement no. 1, 1986, Supplement no. 2, 1997).

EDITIONS AND TRANSLATIONS

The *Lais*

Ewert, Alfred, *Marie de France: Lais* (Oxford: Blackwell, 1944). Reissued with an introduction and bibliography by Glyn S. Burgess (Bristol: Bristol Classical Press, 1995).

Hanning, Robert and Joan Ferrante, *The Lais of Marie de France* (New York: Dutton; Toronto, Vancouver: Clarke, Irwin and Co., 1978, reissued Durham, NC: The Labyrinth Press, 1982). A translation in blank verse.

Harf-Lancner, Laurence, *Lais de Marie de France* (Paris: Le Livre de Poche, 1990). Warnke's text with a facing translation.

Jonin, Pierre, *Les Lais de Marie de France* (Paris: Champion, 1972, 2nd edn, 1978). A French prose translation.

Lods, Jeanne, *Les Lais de Marie de France* (Paris: Champion, 1959).

Mason, Eugene, *French Mediaeval Romances from the Lays of Marie de France* (London: Dent; New York: Dutton, 1911, reprint 1954, further reprint New York: AMS Press, 1976). An English prose translation.

Micha, Alexandre, *Lais de Marie de France, présentés, traduits et annotés* (Paris: GF-Flammarion, 1994). An edition with a facing translation.

Otaka, Yorio, *Marie de France, oeuvres complètes* (Tokio: Maison d'Edition Kazama, 1987).

Rychner, Jean, *Les Lais de Marie de France* (Paris: Champion, 1966, 2nd edn, 1981).

Warnke, Karl, *Die Lais der Marie de France* (Halle: Niemeyer, 1885, 2nd edn, 1900, 3rd edn 1925). Reprint of 3rd edn (Geneva: Slatkine, 1974).

The *Fables*

Brucker, Charles, *Marie de France, Les Fables* (Louvain: Peeters, 1991, 2nd edn, 1998). Includes a facing translation in French.

Martin, Mary Lou, *The Fables of Marie de France: an English Translation* (Birmingham, Alabama: Summa Publications, 1984). Warnke's text with a facing prose translation.

Spiegel, Harriet, *Marie de France: Fables, edited and translated* (Toronto, Buffalo and London: University of Toronto Press, 1987). An edition with a facing verse translation.

Warnke, Karl, *Die Fabeln der Marie de France* (Halle: Niemeyer, 1898; reprint Geneva: Slatkine, 1974).

See also Otaka above.

The *Espurgatoire Seint Patriz*

Curley, Michael J., *Saint Patrick's Purgatory: a Poem by Marie de France, Translated with an Introduction and Notes* (Binghamton, New York: Center for Medieval and Early Renaissance Texts, 1993). Warnke's text with a facing translation in English.

Jenkins, Thomas A., *Marie de France: Espurgatoire Seint Patriz, an Old French Poem of the Twelfth Century* (Philadelphia, 1894, 2nd edn Chicago: University of Chicago Press, 1903; reprint Geneva: Slatkine, 1974).

Pontfarcy, Yolande de, *Marie de France, L'Espurgatoire Seint Patriz: nouvelle édition critique accompagnée du De Purgatorio Sancti Patricii (éd. de Warnke), d'une introduction, d'une traduction, de notes et d'un glossaire* (Louvain and Paris: Peeters, 1995).

Warnke, Karl, *Das Buch vom Espurgatoire S. Patrice der Marie de France und seine Quelle* (Halle: Niemeyer, 1938; reprint Geneva: Slatkine, 1976).

See also Otaka above.

THE IDENTITY OF MARIE DE FRANCE

Fox, John C., 'Marie de France', *English Historical Review*, 25 (1910), 303–6. As the Abbess of Shaftesbury.

— 'Mary, Abbess of Shaftesbury', ibid., 26 (1911), 317–26.

Grillo, Peter R., 'Was Marie de France the Daughter of Waleran II, Count of Meulan?', *Medium Aevum*, 57 (1988), 269–74.

Holmes, Urban T., Jr, 'New Thoughts on Marie de France', *Studies in Philology*, 29 (1932), 1–10. As Marie de Meulan.

Knapton, Antoinette, 'A la Recherche de Marie de France', *Romance Notes*, 19 (1978), 248–53. As Marie de Boulogne.

Levi, Ezio, 'Maria di Francia e le abbazie d'Inghilterra', *Archivum Romanicum*, 5 (1921), 472–93. As a nun from Reading.

Pontfarcy, Yolande de, 'Si Marie de France était Marie de Meulan . . .', *Cahiers de Civilisation Médiévale*, 38 (1995), 353–61.

Winkler, Emil, *Französische Dichter des Mittelalters: II, Marie de France* (Vienna: Hölder, 1918). As Marie de Champagne.

Identifications of Count William (selected)

Ahlström, Axel, *Marie de France et les lais narratifs* (Gothenburg, 1925). As William of Gloucester.

Levi, Ezio, 'Il Re giovane e Maria di Francia', *Archivum Romanicum*, 5 (1921), 448–71. As William Marshal. See also for the 'nobles reis' as Henri au Cort Mantel.

Painter, Sidney, 'To whom were dedicated the *Fables* of Marie de France?', *Modern Language Notes*, 48 (1933), 367–9. Reprinted in *Feudalism and Liberty* (Baltimore: Johns Hopkins Press, 1961), 108–10. As William of Mandeville.

Soudée, Madeleine, 'Le Dédicataire des *Ysopets* de Marie de France', *Les Lettres Modernes*, 35 (1981), 183–98. As William Marshal.

GENERAL STUDIES ON MARIE DE FRANCE

Books

Baum, Richard, *Recherches sur les oeuvres attribuées à Marie de France* (Heidelberg: Winter, 1968).

Boland, Margaret M., *Architectural Structure in the Lais of Marie de France* (New York: Lang, 1996).

Burgess, Glyn S., *The Lais of Marie de France: Text and Context* (Athens, Georgia: University of Georgia Press; Manchester: Manchester University Press, 1987).

Clifford, Paula, *Marie de France: Lais* (London: Grant and Cutler, 1982).

Dufournet, Jean (ed.), *Amour et merveille: les Lais de Marie de France* (Paris: Champion, 1995).

Hoepffner, Ernest, *Les Lais de Marie de France* (Paris: Boivin, 1935; reprint Paris: Nizet, 1966).

Joubert, Claude-Henry, *Oyez ke dit Marie: étude sur les Lais de Marie de France (XIIe siècle)* (Paris: Corti, 1987).

Kroll, Renate, *Der narrative Lai als eigenständige Gattung in der Literatur des Mittelalters: zum Strukturprincip der Aventure in den Lais* (Tübingen: Niemeyer, 1984).

McClelland, Denise, *Le Vocabulaire des Lais de Marie de France* (Ottawa: Université d'Ottawa, 1977)

Maréchal, Chantal A. (ed.), *In Quest of Marie de France: a Twelfth-Century Poet* (Lewiston, Queenston and Lampeter: The Edwin Mellen Press, 1992).

Ménard, Philippe, *Les Lais de Marie de France: contes d'amour et d'aventure du moyen âge* (Paris: Presses Universitaires de France, 1979, 2nd edn 1995).

Mickel, Emanuel J., Jr, *Marie de France* (New York: Twayne, 1974).

Mikhaïlova, Milena. *Le Présent de Marie* (Paris, New York and Amsterdam: Diderot, 1996).

Ringger, Kurt, *Die Lais: zur Struktur der dichterischen Einbildungskraft der Marie de France* (Tübingen: Niemeyer, 1973).

Rothschild, Judith R., *Narrative Technique in the Lais of Marie de France: Themes and Variations*, vol. I (Chapel Hill: University of North Carolina Press, 1974).

Sienaert, Edgard, *Les Lais de Marie de France: du conte merveilleux à la nouvelle psychologique* (Paris: Champion, 1978).

Selected Articles

Bowers, John M., 'Ordeals, Privacy, and the *Lais* of Marie de France', *Journal of Medieval and Renaissance Studies*, 24 (1994), 1–31.

Bruckner, Matilda T., 'Strategies of Naming in Marie de France's *Lais*: at the Crossroads of Gender and Genre', *Neophilologus*, 75 (1991), 31–40.

Bullock-Davies, Constance, 'Marie de France: a Reassessment of her Narrative Technique in the *Lais*', in *Court and Poet: Selected Proceedings of the Third Congress of the International Courtly Literature Society (Liverpool 1980)*, ed. G. S. Burgess (Liverpool: Francis Cairns, 1981), 93–9.

Damon, S. Foster, 'Marie de France: Psychologist of Courtly Love', *Publications of the Modern Language Association of America*, 44 (1929), 968–96.

De Caluwé, Jacques, 'L'Elément chrétien dans les *Lais* de Marie de France', in *Mélanges de littérature du moyen âge au XXe siècle offerts à Mademoiselle Jeanne Lods*, 2 vols (Paris: Ecole Normale de Jeunes Filles, 1978), I, 95–114.

Dubuis. Roger, 'La notion de *druerie* dans les *Lais* de Marie de France', *Le Moyen Age*, 98 (1992), 391–413.

Flori, Jean, 'Amour et société aristocratique au XIIe siècle: l'exemple des *Lais* de Marie de France', *Le Moyen Age*, 98 (1992), 17–34.

— 'Aristocratie et valeurs "chevaleresques" dans la seconde moitié du XIIᵉ siècle: l'exemple des *Lais* de Marie de France', *Le Moyen Age*, 96 (1990), 35–65.

— 'Seigneurie, noblesse et chevalerie dans les *Lais* de Marie de France', *Romania*, 108 (1987), 183–206.

Foulet, Lucien, 'Marie de France et les lais bretons', *Zeitschrift für romanische Philologie*, (1905), 19–56, 293–322.

Francis, Elizabeth A., 'Marie de France et son temps', *Romania*, 72 (1951), 78–99.

Frappier, Jean, 'Remarques sur la structure du lai: essai de définition et de classement', in *La Littérature narrative d'imagination, des genres littéraires aux techniques d'expression* (Paris: Presses Universitaires de France, 1961), pp. 23–39.

Freeman, Michelle A., 'Marie de France's Poetics of Silence: the Implications for a Feminine Translation', *Publications of the Modern Language Association of America*, 99 (1984), 860–83.

Guidot, Bernard, 'Pouvoirs et séduction, pouvoir de séduction dans les *Lais* de Marie de France', *Romanische Forschungen*, 102 (1990), 425–33.

Hoepffner, Ernest, 'Pour la cronologie des *Lais* de Marie de France', *Romania*, 59 (1933), 351–70, 60 (1934), 36–66.

— 'La Géographie et l'histoire dans les *Lais* de Marie de France', *Romania*, 56 (1930), 1–32.

Hunt, Tony, 'Glossing Marie de France', *Romanische Forschungen*, 86 (1974), 396–418.

Illingworth, Richard N., 'La Chronologie des *Lais* de Marie de France', *Romania*, 87 (1966), 433–75.

Jonin, Pierre, 'Le *Je* de Marie de France dans les *Lais*', *Romania*, 103 (1982), 170–86.

Knapton, Antoinette, 'La Structure en triptyque des *Lais de Marie de France*', *Revue du Pacifique*, 3 (1977), 87–92.

McCulloch, Florence, 'Length, Recitation and Meaning of the *Lais* of Marie de France', *Kentucky Romance Quarterly*, 25 (1978), 257–68.

Mickel, Emanuel J., Jr, 'A Reconsideration of the *Lais* of Marie de France', *Speculum*, 46 (1971), 39–65.

Nelson, Jan A., 'Abbreviated Style and *Les Lais de Marie de France*', *Romance Quarterly*, (1992), 131–44.

Nichols, Stephen G., 'Marie de France's Commonplaces', *Yale French Studies*, special issue, 1991, 134–48.

Ollier, Marie-Louise, 'Les *Lais* de Marie de France ou le recueil comme forme', in *La Nouvelle: actes du colloque international de Montréal (McGill University, 14–16 octobre 1982)*, eds M. Picone, G. Di Stefano and P.M. Stewart (Montreal: Plato Academic Press, 1984), 64–9.

Pickens, Rupert T., 'History and Meaning in the *Lais* of Marie de France', in *Studies on the Seven Sages of Rome and Other Essays in Medieval Literature Dedicated to the Memory of Jean Misrahi* (Honolulu: Educational Research Associates, 1978), 201–11.

— 'La Poétique de Marie de France d'après les prologues des *Lais*', *Les Lettres Romanes*, 32 (1978), 367–84.

Rieger, Dietmar, 'Evasion et conscience des problèmes dans les *Lais* de Marie de France', *Spicilegio Moderno*, 12 (1979), 49–69.

Semple, Benjamin, 'The Male Psyche and the Female Sacred Body in Marie de France and Christine de Pizan', *Yale French Studies*, 86 (1994), 164–86.

Smithers, G. V., 'Story-Patterns in Some Breton Lays', *Medium Aevum*, 22 (1953), 61–92.

Spitzer, Leo, 'Marie de France – Dichterin von Problem-Märchen', *Zeitschrift für romanische Philologie*, 50 (1930), 29–67.

— 'The Prologue to the *Lais* of Marie de France and Medieval Poetics', *Modern Philology*, 41 (1943–4), 96–102. Reprinted in *Romanische Literaturstudien 1936–1956* (Tübingen: Niemeyer, 1959), 8–14.

Sturges, Robert, 'Texts and Readers in Marie de France's *Lais*', *Romanic Review*, 71 (1980), 244–64.

Vitz, Evelyn B., 'The *Lais* of Marie de France: "Narrative Grammar" and the Literary Text', *Romanic Review*, 74 (1983), 383–404. Reprinted in *Medieval Narrative and Modern Narratology: Subjects and Objects of Desire* (New York and London: New York University Press, 1989), 149–75.

— 'Orality, Literacy and the Early Tristan Material: Beroul, Thomas, Marie de France', *Romanic Review*, 78 (1987), 299–310.

For studies dealing with individual lays see Burgess, revised edition of A. Ewert, *Marie de France: Lais*, lviii–lxxii.

INDEX OF
PROPER NAMES

This list does not include eponymous characters or titles of lays.

Aaron, St. *Yonec,* p. 92. A Romano-British saint, martyred during the persecutions of Diocletian (third century A.D.).

Adam. *Yonec,* p. 88.

Alexandrian. *Guigemar,* p. 45, *Lanval,* p. 74. Used to describe the provenance of expensive fabrics.

Anjou. *Guigemar,* p. 44, *Chaitivel,* p. 106.

Arthur, King. *Lanval,* p. 73 ff.

Avalon. *Lanval,* p. 81. The home of Lanval's fairy mistress.

Barfleur. *Milun,* p. 108. Port near Cherbourg in Normandy.

Boulogne. *Chaitivel,* p. 106.

Brabant. *Chaitivel,* p. 106. An independent Duchy, in the lowlands of what is now the Netherlands and Belgium.

Brenguein. *Chevrefoil,* p. 110. Iseult's maid-servant.

Breton (language). *Bisclavret,* p. 68, *Lanval,* p. 73.

Breton lay. *Eliduc,* p. 111.

Bretons (inhabitants). *Guigemar,* p. 43, *Equitan,* pp. 56, 60, *Lanval,* p. 81, *Deus Amanz,* pp. 82, 85, *Laüstic,* p. 94, 96, *Milun,* p. 102, *Eliduc,* p. 126.

Britain. *Yonec,* p. 86.

Brittany. *Guigemar,* pp. 43, 47, 51, 52, *Equitan,* p. 56, *Le Fresne,* pp. 61, 64, *Bisclavret,* pp. 68, 71, *Milun,* pp. 101, 102, 104, *Chaitivel,* p. 105, *Eliduc,* p.111.

Burgundy. *Guigemar,* p. 44.

Caerleon (Gwent). *Yonec,* p. 42, *Milun,* p. 99.

Caerwent (Gwent). *Yonec,* pp. 86, 92.

Carlisle (Cumbria). *Lanval,* p. 73.

Clement, St. *Eliduc,* p. 121. Refers to Pope Clement I (died *c.* 99 A.D.), who preserved the life of a child which had been submerged in the sea for a whole year.

Codre, La. *Le Fresne*, p. 65 ff. The twin sister of Le Fresne.
Constantinople. *Le Fresne*, p. 62.
Cornwall. *Chevrefoil*, p. 109.
Cornwall, Count of. *Lanval*, p. 78.

Dol. *Le Fresne*, p. 64. Town in Upper Brittany.
Dol, Archbishop of. *Le Fresne*, p. 65 ff.
Duelas. *Yonec*, p. 86. The river on which Marie situates the town of Caerwent.

Easter. *Milun*, p. 102, *Chaitivel*, p. 106.
England. *Milun*, p. 97 (see **Logres**).
English(language). *Laüstic*, p. 94.
English(men). *Milun*, p. 102, *Chevrefoil*, p. 110.
Exeter. *Eliduc*, p. 112.

Flanders. *Guigemar*, p. 43, *Chaitivel*, p. 106.
Flemish. *Milun*, p. 102, *Chaitivel*, p. 106.
Four Sorrows, The. *Chaitivel*, pp. 105, 108. Alternative title for poem.
French (language). *Prologue*, p. 41, *Laüstic*, p. 94.
French (inhabitants). *Milun*, p. 102, *Chaitivel*, p. 106. *Chevrefoil*, p. 110.

Garwaf. *Bisclavret*, p. 68. Norman title for poem.
Gascony. *Guigemar*, p. 44.
Gawain. *Lanval*, pp. 76, 78.
Gotelef. *Chevrefoil*, p. 110. English title for poem.
Gotland. *Milun*, p. 97. The form in the text is *Guhtlande*. Seems to refer either to the Swedish island of Gotland in the Baltic Sea or to the Danish peninsula, Jutland (Jylland).
Guildelüec. *Eliduc*, p. 111 ff. First wife of Eliduc.
Guildelüec and Guilliadun. *Eliduc*, p. 111. Alternative title for *Eliduc*.
Guilliadun. *Eliduc*, p. 111 ff. Second wife of Eliduc.
Gurun. *Le Fresne*, p. 64 ff. Lover, later husband, of Le Fresne.

Hainault. *Chaitivel*, p. 106. Now a province in south-west Belgium.
Hoilas. *Guigemar*, p. 43. King of Brittany. Probably to be identified as Hoël. Several Breton leaders bore this name, but none seems to have had the title King.

Ireland. *Milun*, p. 97.
Iwain. *Lanval*, pp. 76, 80.

John, St. *Lanval*, p. 76. St John's Day is 24 June.

Latin. *Prologue*, p. 41.

Liun. *Guigemar*, p. 43. Modern St Pol-de-Léon and surrounding area, *département* of Finistère.

Logres. *Lanval*, p. 73, *Eliduc*, pp. 112, 124. England.

Lorraine. *Guigemar*, p. 44.

Love (personified). *Guigemar*, p. 49, *Equitan*, p. 57, *Lanval*, p. 74, *Eliduc*, p. 115.

Marie. *Guigemar*, p. 43. Author of the twelve lays.

Mary, Virgin. *Eliduc*, p. 121.

Mark, King. *Chevrefoil*, pp. 109, 110.

Meriaduc. *Guigemar*, p. 52 ff. Breton knight, Guigemar's friend, then adversary.

Mont St Michel. *Milun*, p. 102.

Muldumarec. *Yonec*, p. 86 ff. Yonec's father.

Nantes. *Equitan*, p. 56, *Chaitivel*, pp. 105, 106. The interpretation 'Lord of Nantes' for 'Sire des Nauns' in *Equitan*, v. 12, is not certain.

Nature. *Guigemar*, p. 44, *Equitan*, p. 56, *Le Fresne*, p. 64.

Neustria. *Deus Amanz*, p. 82. Former name for Normandy.

Nicholas, St. *Eliduc*, p. 121. Patron saint of sailors beset by storms (for having saved doomed mariners off the coast of Lycia).

Nightingale. *Laüstic*, p. 94. Alternative title for poem.

Noguent. *Guigemar*, p. 43. Sister of Guigemar.

Normandy. *Deus Amanz*, p. 82, *Milun*, p. 102.

Norman(s). *Bisclavret*, p. 68, *Milun*, p. 102, *Chaitivel*, p. 106.

Northumbria. *Milun*, pp. 98, 103.

Norway. *Milun*, p. 97.

Octavian, Emperor. *Lanval*, p. 74. The Emperor Augustus.

Oridial. *Guigemar*, p. 43. Guigemar's father.

Ovid. *Guigemar*, p. 46. The book which Venus is depicted as throwing into the fire is normally interpreted as the *Remedia Amoris*, but the reference could be to the *Ars Amatoria* or to the entire Ovidian system.

Peerless One, The. *Milun*, p. 101. The name given to Milun's son.

Pentecost. *Lanval*, p. 73, *Chevrefoil*, p. 109.

Phrygian. *Lanval*, p. 79. Designates the provenance of a type of silk.

Picts. *Lanval*, p. 73.

Pistrians. *Deux Amanz*, p. 82. Inhabitants of Pitres.

Pitres. *Deus Amanz*, p. 82. Town not far from Rouen.

Pitres, Valley of. *Deus Amanz*, p. 82.

Priscian. *Prologue*, p. 41. The early sixth-century A.D. Latin grammarian Priscianus Caesariensis. Marie's reference may be to his best-known work, the *Institutiones Grammaticae*, but could be to remarks made in his *Prae-exercitamina*.

Quatre Deuls, Les. *Chaitivel*, p. 105. Alternative title for the poem.

Rossignol. *Laüstic*, p. 94. The French title for the poem.

Round Table, The. *Lanval*, p. 73.

St Malo. *Laüstic*, p. 94. The area surrounding the town of St Malo in Brittany.

Salerno. *Deus Amanz*, p. 83. Town in Campania (Italy) with a famous medical school.

Scotland. *Milun*, p. 97. Occurs in text as *Albanie* 'Albany'.

Scots. *Lanval*, p. 73.

Seine, River. *Deus Amanz*, p. 84.

Semiramis. *Lanval*, p. 74. The partly historical, partly mythical Queen Sammuramat (ninth century B.C.), queen of Assyria.

Solomon. *Guigemar*, p. 45. The expression in the text is '*a l'ovre Salemun*' (v. 173). 'Solomon's work' seems to be associated with his Temple and to designate ancient Byzantine work in the form of carving in bas-relief overlaid with gold.

Southampton. *Milun*, p. 101.

South Wales. *Milun*, p. 97, *Chevrefoil*, p. 109. See **Wales**.

Spanish. *Lanval*, p. 79. Used to designate a breed of mule.

Tintagel. *Chevrefoil*, p. 109. Residence of King Mark in Cornwall.

Totnes (Devon). *Eliduc*, pp. 112, 121.

Tristram. *Chevrefoil*, pp. 109, 110.

Two Lovers, Mountain of the. *Deus Amanz*, p. 85.

Unhappy One, The. *Chaitivel*, pp. 105, 108. Alternative title for the poem.

Venus. *Guigemar*, p. 46.

Wales. *Milun*, p. 103, *Chevrefoil*, p. 110. See South Wales.

LANVAL

L'aventure d'un autre lai,
Cum ele avient, vus cunterai.
Fait fu d'un mut gentil vassal;
En bretans l'apelent *Lanval*.   4
A Kardoel surjurnot li reis,
Artur li pruz e li curteis,
Pur les Escoz e pur les Pis
Que destrueient le païs;   8
En la tere de Logre entroënt
E mut suvent la damagoënt.
A la Pentecuste en esté
I aveit li reis sujurné;   12
Asez i duna riches duns,
E as cuntes e as baruns.
A ceus de la Table Roünde
– N'ot tant de teus en tut le munde –   16
Femmes e tere departi,
Par tut, fors un ki l'ot servi.
Ceo fu Lanval; ne l'en sovient
Ne nul des soens bien ne li tient.   20
Pur sa valur, pur sa largesce,
Pur sa beauté, pur sa pruësce,
L'envioënt tut li plusur.
Tel li mustra semblant d'amur,   24
S'al chevalier mesavenist,
Ja une feiz ne l'en pleinsist.
Fiz a rei fu, de haut parage,
Mes luin ert de sun heritage.   28
De la meisnee le rei fu;
Tut sun aveir ad despendu,
Kar li reis rien ne li dona

Ne Lanval ne li demanda.   32
Ore est Lanval mut entrepris,
Mut est dolent, mut pensis.
Seignurs, ne vus esmerveillez,
Hume estrange descunseillez   36
Mut est dolent en autre tere,
Quant il ne seit u sucurs quere.
Le chevalier dunt jeo vus di,
Que tant aveit le rei servi,   40
Un jur munta sur sun destrer,
Si s'est alez esbaneer.
Fors de la vile est eissuz,
Tut sul est en un pré venuz.   44
Sur une ewe curaunt descent,
Mes sis cheval tremble forment.
Il le descengle, si s'en vait,
En mi le pré vuiltrer le lait.   48
Le pan de sun mantel plia
Desuz sun chief, puis se cucha.
Mut est pensis pur sa mesaise,
Il ne veit chose ki li plaise.   52
La u il gist en teu maniere,
Garda aval lez la riviere,
Si vit venir deus dameiseles.
Unc n'en ot veü plus beles.   56
Vestues ierent richement,
Laciees mut estreitement
En deus blians de purpre bis;
Mut par aveient bel le vis.   60
L'eisnee portout uns bacins,
Doré furent, bien faiz e fins,
Le veir vus en dirai sanz faile.
L'autre portout une tuaile.   64
Eles s'en sunt alees dreit
La u li chevaler giseit.
Lanval, que mut fu enseigniez,
Cuntre eles s'en levad en piez.   68
Celes l'unt primes salué,
Lur message li unt cunté:

'Sire Lanval, ma dameisele,
Que tant est pruz e sage e bele, 72
Ele nus enveie pur vus;
Kar i venez ensemble od nus.
Sauvement vus i cundurums;
Veez, pres est li paveilluns.' 76
Li chevalers od eles vait,
De sun cheval ne tient nul plait,
Que devant li pesseit al pré.
Treske al tref l'unt amené, 80
Que mut fu beaus e bien asis.
La reïne Semiramis,
Quant ele ot unkes plus aveir
E plus pussaunce e plus saveir, 84
Ne l'emperere Octovïen,
N'esligasent le destre pan.
Un aigle d'or ot desus mis,
De cel ne sai dire le pris, 88
Ne des cordes ne des peissuns
Que del tref tienent les giruns.
Suz ciel n'ad rei kis esligast
Pur nul aver k'il i donast. 92
Dedenz cel tref fu la pucele;
Flur de lis e rose nuvele,
Quant ele pert al tens d'esté,
Trespassot ele de beauté. 96
Ele jut sur un lit mut bel
– Li drap valeient un chastel –
En sa chemise senglement;
Mut ot le cors bien fait e gent. 100
Un cher mantel de blanc hermine,
Covert de purpre alexandrine,
Ot pur le chaut sur li geté.
Tut ot descovert le costé, 104
Le vis, le col e la peitrine;
Plus ert blanche que flur d'espine.
Le chevaler avant ala,
E la pucele l'apela. 108
Il s'est devant le lit asis.

'Lanval', fet ele, 'beus amis,
Pur vus vienc jeo fors de ma tere;
De luinz vus sui venue quere.   112
Se vus estes pruz e curteis,
Emperere ne quens ne reis
N'ot unkes tant joie ne bien,
Kar jo vus aim sur tute rien.'   116
Il l'esgarda, si la vit bele;
Amurs le puint de l'estencele
Que sun quor alume e esprent.
Il li respunt avenantment: 120
'Bele', fet il, 'si vus pleiseit
E cele joie me aveneit
Que vus me vousissez amer,
Ne savrïez rien comander   124
Que jeo ne face a mien poeir,
Turt a folie u a saveir.
Jeo ferai voz comandemenz;
Pur vus guerpirai tutes genz.   128
Jamés ne queor de vus partir;
Ceo est la rien que plus desir.'
Quant la meschine oï parler
Celui que tant la peot amer,   132
S'amur e sun cors li otreie.
Ore est Lanval en dreite veie!
Un dun li ad duné aprés:
Ja cele rien ne vudra mes   136
Que il nen ait a sun talent.
Doinst e despende largement,
Ele li troverat asez.
Mut est Lanval bien herbergez: 140
Cum plus despendra richement,
Plus averat or e argent.
'Amis', fet ele, 'ore vus chasti,
Si vus comant e si vus pri;   144
Ne vus descovrez a nul humme.
De ceo vus dirai ja la summe,
A tuz jurs m'avrïez perdue,
Si ceste amur esteit seüe.   148

Jamés ne me purriez veeir
Ne de mun cors seisine aveir.'
Il li respunt que bien tendra
Ceo que ele li comaundera. 152
Delez li s'est el lit cuchiez.
Ore est Lanval bien herbergez!
Ensemble od li la relevee
Demurat tresque a la vespree, 156
E plus i fust, se il poïst
E s'amie lui cunsentist.
'Amis', fet ele, 'levez sus.
Vus n'i poëz demurer plus; 160
Alez vus en, jeo remeindrai.
Mes une chose vus dirai:
Quant vus vodrez od mei parler,
Ja ne savrez cel liu penser 164
U nuls puïst aver sa amie
Sanz repreoce, sanz vileinie,
Que jeo ne vus seie en present
A fere tut vostre talent. 168
Nul hum fors vus ne me verra
Ne ma parole nen orra.'
Quant il l'oï, mut en fu liez;
Il la baisa, puis s'est dresciez. 172
Celes que al tref l'amenerent
De riches dras le cunreerent;
Quant il fu vestu de nuvel,
Suz ciel nen ot plus bel dancel. 176
N'esteit mie fous ne vileins.
L'ewe li donent a ses meins
E la tuaille a essuer.
Puis li aportent a manger; 180
Od s'amie prist le super.
Ne feseit mie a refuser.
Mut fu servi curteisement
E il a grant joie le prent. 184
Un entremés i ot plener,
Que mut pleiseit al chevalier,
Kar s'amie baisout sovent

E acolot estreitement.   188
Quant del manger furent levé,
Sun cheval li unt amené;
Bien li unt la sele mise.
Mut ad trové riche servise.   192
Il prent cungé, si est muntez,
Vers la cité s'en est alez.
Suvent esgarde ariere sei;
Mut est Lanval en grant esfrei.   196
De s'aventure vait pensaunt
E en sun curage dotaunt.
Esbaïz est, ne seit que creire,
Il ne la quide mie a veire.   200
Il est a sun ostel venuz;
Ses hummes treve bien vestuz.
Icele nuit bon ostel tient,
Mes nul ne sot dunt ceo li vient.   204
N'ot en la vile chevalier
Ki de surjur ait grant mestier
Que il ne face a lui venir
E richement e bien servir.   208
Lanval donout les riches duns,
Lanval aquitout les prisuns,
Lanval vesteit les jugleürs,
Lanval feseit les granz honurs.   212
N'i ot estrange ne privé
A ki Lanval n'eüst doné.
Mut ot Lanval joie e deduit:
U seit par jur u seit par nuit,   216
S'amie peot veer sovent,
Tut est a sun comandement.
Ceo m'est avis, meïsmes l'an,
Aprés la feste seint Johan,   220
D'ici qu'a trente chevalier
S'ierent alé esbanïer
En un vergier desuz la tur,
U la reïne ert a surjur.   224
Ensemble od eus esteit Walwains
E sis cusins, li beaus Ywains.

E dist Walwains, li francs, li pruz,
Que tant se fist amer de tuz: 228
'Par Deu, segnurs, nus feimes mal
De nostre cumpainun Lanval,
Que tant est larges e curteis,
E sis peres est riches reis,   232
Qu'od nus ne l'avum amené.'
A tant sunt ariere turné;
A sun ostel revient ariere,
Lanval ameinent par preere.   236
A une fenestre entaillie
S'esteit la reïne apuïe.
Treis dames ot ensemble od li.
La maisnie le rei choisi,   240
Lanval conut e esgarda.
Une des dames apela;
Par li manda ses dameiseles,
Les plus quointes e les plus beles.   244
Od li s'irrunt esbanïer
La u cil erent al vergier.
Trente en menat od li e plus;
Par les degrez descendent jus.   248
Les chevalers encuntre vunt,
Que pur eles grant joie unt.
Il les unt prises par les mains;
Cil parlemenz n'iert pas vilains.   252
Lanval s'en vait a une part
Mut luin des autres; ceo li est tart
Que s'amie puïst tenir,
Baiser, acoler e sentir.   256
L'autrui joie prise petit,
Si il nen ad le suen delit.
Quant la reïne sul le veit,
Al chevaler en va tut dreit;   260
Lunc lui s'asist, si l'apela,
Tut sun curage li mustra:
'Lanval, mut vus ai honuré
E mut cheri e mut amé.   264
Tute m'amur poëz aveir.

Kar me dites vostre voleir.
Ma druërie vus otrei;
Mut devez estre lié de mei.'
'Dame', fet il, 'lessez m'ester.   268
Jeo n'ai cure de vus amer.
Lungement ai servi le rei;
Ne li voil pas mentir ma fei.
Ja pur vus ne pur vostre amur   272
Ne mesferai a mun seignur.'
La reïne s'en curuça,
Irïe fu, si mesparla:
'Lanval', fet ele, 'bien le quit.   276
Vus n'amez gueres cel delit.
Asez le m'ad hum dit sovent
Que des femmez n'avez talent.
Vallez avez bien afeitiez,   280
Ensemble od eus vus deduiez.
Vileins cuarz, mauveis failliz,
Mut est mi sires maubailliz,
Que pres de lui vus ad suffert;   284
Mun escïent que Deus en pert.'
Quant il l'oï, mut fu dolent,
Del respundre ne fu pas lent.
Teu chose dist par maltalent   288
Dunt il se repenti sovent.
'Dame', dist il, 'de cel mestier
Ne me sai jeo nïent aidier;
Mes jo aim e si sui amis   292
Cele ke deit aver le pris
Sur tutes celes que jeo sai.
E une chose vus dirai,   296
Bien le sachez a descovert:
Une de celes ki la sert,
Tute la plus povre meschine,
Vaut meuz de vus, dame reïne,   300
De cors, de vis e de beauté,
D'enseignement e de bunté.'
La reïne s'en part a tant,
En sa chambre en vait plurant.   304

Mut fu dolente e curuciee
De ceo k'il out si avilee.
En sun lit malade cucha;
Jamés, ceo dit, ne levera,   308
Si li reis ne l'en feseit dreit
De ceo dunt ele se pleindreit.
Li reis fu del bois repeiriez,
Mut out le jur esté haitiez,   312
As chambres la reïne entra.
Quant el le vit, si se clamma;
As piez li chiet, merci li crie,
E dit que Lanval l'ad hunie: 316
De druërie la requist;
Pur ceo que ele l'en escundist,
Mut la laidi e avila.
De tele amie se vanta,   320
Que tant iert cuinte e noble e fiere,
Que meuz valut sa chamberere,
La plus povre que tant serveit,
Que la reïne ne feseit.   324
Li reis s'en curuçat forment,
Juré en ad sun serment;
S'il ne s'en peot en curt defendre,
Il le ferat arder u pendre.   328
Fors de la chambre eissi li reis,
De ses baruns apelat treis;
Il les enveie pur Lanval,
Que asez ad dolur e mal.   332
A sun chastel fu revenuz;
Il s'esteit bien aparceüz
Qu'il aveit perdue s'amie;
Descovert ot la drüerie.   336
En une chambre fu tut suls,
Pensis esteit e anguissus;
S'amie apele mut sovent,
Mes ceo ne li valut neent.   340
Il se pleigneit e suspirot,
D'ures en autres se pasmot.
Puis li crie cent feiz merci,

Que ele parolt a sun ami.
Sun quor e sa buche maudit;
C'est merveille k'il ne s'ocit.
Il ne seit tant crier ne braire
Ne debatre ne sei detraire
Que ele en veulle merci aveir,
Sul tant que la puisse veeir.
Oi las, cument se cuntendra?
Cil ke li reis ci enveia,
Il sunt venu, si li unt dit
Que a la curt voise sanz respit.
Li reis l'aveit par eus mandé,
La reïne l'out encusé.
Lanval i vet od sun grant doel.
Il l'eüssent ocis sun veoil.
Il est devant le rei venu,
Mut fu dolent, taisanz e mu,
De grant dolur mustre semblant.
Li reis li dit par maltalant:
'Vassal, vus me avez mut mesfait;
Trop començastes vilein plait
De mei hunir e aviler
E la reïne ledengier.
Vanté vus estes de folie:
Trop par est noble vostre amie,
Quant plus est bele sa meschine
E plus vaillanz que la reïne.'
Lanval defent la deshonur
E la hunte de sun seignur
De mot en mot si cum il dist,
Que la reïne ne requist.
Mes de ceo dunt il ot parlé
Reconut il la verité,
De l'amur dunt il se vanta;
Dolent en est, perdue l'a.
De ceo lur dit qu'il en ferat
Quanque la curz esgarderat.
Li reis fu mut vers li irez;
Tuz ses hummes ad enveiez

344

348

352

356

360

364

368

372

376

380

Pur dire dreit qu'il en deit faire,
Qu'um ne li puisse a mal retraire. 384
Cil unt sun commandement fait,
U eus seit bel u eus seit lait.
Comunement i sunt alé
E unt jugé e esgardé 388
Que Lanval deit aveir un jur;
Mes plegges truisse a sun seignur
Qu'il atendra sun jugement
E revendra en sun present, 392
Si serat la curt esforciee
Kar n'i ot dunc fors la maisnee.
Al rei revienent li barun,
Si li mustrerent la reisun. 396
Li reis ad plegges demandé.
Lanval fu sul e esgaré,
N'i aveit parent ne ami.
Walwain i vait, ki l'a plevi 400
E tuit si cumpainun aprés.
Li reis lur dit: 'E jol vus les
Sur quanke vus tenez de mei,
Teres e fieus, chescun par sei'. 404
Quant plevi fu, dunc n'i ot el.
Alez s'en est a sun ostel.
Li chevaler l'unt conveé;
Mut l'unt blasmé e chastïé 408
K'il ne face si grant dolur,
E maudïent si fol' amur.
Chescun jur l'aloënt veer,
Pur ceo k'il voleient saveir 412
U il beüst u il mangast;
Mut dotouent k'il s'afolast.
Al jur que cil orent numé
Li barun furent asemblé. 416
Li reis e la reïne i fu,
E li plegge unt Lanval rendu.
Mut furent tuz pur li dolent;
Jeo quid k'il en i ot teus cent 420
Ki feïssent tut lur poeir

Pur lui sanz pleit delivre aveir.
Il iert retté a mut grant tort.
Li reis demande le recort   424
Sulunc le cleim e les respuns;
Ore est trestut sur les baruns.
Il sunt al jugement alé.
Mut sunt pensifs e esgaré   428
Del franc humme d'autre païs
Que entre eus ert si entrepris.
Encumbrer le veulent plusur
Pur la volenté sun seignur.   432
Ceo dist li quoens de Cornwaille:
'Ja endreit nuls n'i avra faille,
Kar ki que en plurt e ki que en chant,
Le dreit estuet aler avant.   436
Li reis parla vers sun vassal
Que jeo vus oi numer Lanval;
De felunie le retta
E d'un mesfait l'acheisuna,   440
D'un' amur dunt il se vanta
E ma dame s'en curuça.
Nuls ne l'apele fors le rei.
Par cele fei ke jeo vus dei,   444
Ki bien en veut dire le veir,
Ja n'i deüst respuns aveir
Si pur ceo nun que a sun seignur
Deit hum bien par tut faire honur.   448
Un serement l'en gagera
E li reis le nus pardura.
E s'il peot aver sun guarant
E s'amie venist avant,   452
E ceo fust veir k'il en deïst,
Dunt la reïne se marist,
De ceo avra il bien merci,
Quant pur vilté nel dist de li.   456
E s'il ne peot garant aveir,
Ceo li devum faire saveir:
Tut sun servise perde del rei
E sil deit cungeer de sei.'   460

Al chevaler unt enveé
E si li unt dit e nuntié
Que s'amie face venir
Pur lui tencer e garentir.   464
Il lur dit que il ne poeit,
Ja pur li sucurs nen avreit.
Cil s'en revunt as jugeürs
Ki n'i atendent nul sucurs.   468
Li reis les hastot durement
Pur la reïne, kis atent.
Quant il deveient departir,
Deus puceles virent venir   472
Sur deus beaus palefreiz amblanz.
Mut par esteient avenanz;
De cendal purpre sunt vestues
Tut senglement a lur char nues.   476
Cil les esgardent volenters.
Walwain, od lui treis chevalers,
Vait a Lanval, si li cunta,
Les deus puceles li mustra.   480
Mut fu haitié, forment li prie
Qu'il li deïst si c'ert s'amie.
Il lur ad dit ne seit ki sunt
Ne dunt vienent ne u eles vunt.   484
Celes sunt alees avant
Tut a cheval; par tel semblant
Descendirent devant le deis,
La u seeit Artur li reis.   488
Eles furent de grant beuté,
Si unt curteisement parlé:
'Reis, fai tes chambres delivrer
E de palies encurtiner   492
U ma dame puïst descendre,
Ensemble od vus veut ostel prendre.'
Il lur otria volenters,
Si appela deus chevalers;   496
As chambres les menerent sus.
A cele feiz ne distrent plus.
Li reis demande a ses baruns

Le jugement e les respuns,   500
E dit que mut l'unt curucié
De ceo que tant l'unt delaié.
'Sire', funt il, 'nus departimes
Pur les dames que nus veïmes;   504
Nus n'i avum nul esgart fait.
Ore recumencerum le plait.'
Dunc assemblerent tut pensif;
Asez i ot noise e estrif.   508
Quant il ierent en cel esfrei,
Deus puceles de gent cunrei,
Vestues de deus pailes freis
– Chevauchent deus muls espanneis –   512
Virent venir la rue aval.
Grant joie en eurent li vassal;
Entre eus dïent qu'ore est gariz
Lanval li pruz e li hardiz.   516
Yweins i est a lui alez,
Ses cumpainuns i ad menez.
'Sire', fet il, 'rehaitiez vus,
Pur amur Deu, parlez od nus!   520
Ici vienent deus dameiseles,
Mut acesmees e mut beles:
C'est vostre amie vereiment.'
Lanval respunt hastivement   524
E dit qu'il pas nes avuot
N'il nes cunut ne nes amot.
A tant furent celes venues,
Devant le rei sunt descendues.   528
Mut les loërent li plusor
De cors, de vis e de colur;
N'i ad cele meuz ne vausist
Que unkes la reïne ne fist.   532
L'aisnee fu curteise e sage;
Avenantment dist sun message:
'Reis, kar nus fai chambres baillier
A oés ma dame herbergier.   536
Ele vient ci a tei parler.'
Il les cumande a mener

Od les autres que anceis vindrent.
Unkes des muls nul plaid ne tindrent.   540
Quant il fu d'eles delivrez,
Puis ad tuz ses baruns mandez
Que le jugement seit renduz.
Trop ad le jur esté tenuz;   544
La reïne s'en curuceit,
Que si lunges les atendeit.
Ja departissent a itant,
Quant par la vile vient errant   548
Tut a cheval une pucele;
En tut le secle n'ot plus bele.
Un blanc palefrei chevachot,
Que bel e suëf la portot;   552
Mut ot bien fet e col e teste,
Suz ciel nen ot plus bele beste.
Riche atur ot al palefrei;
Suz ciel nen ad quens ne rei   556
Ki tut le peüst eslegier
Sanz tere vendre u engagier.
Ele iert vestue en itel guise
De chainsil blanc e de chemise,   560
Que tuz les costez li pareient,
Que de deus parz laciez esteient.
Le cors ot gent, basse la hanche,
Le col plus blanc que neif sur branche;   564
Les oilz ot vairs e blanc le vis,
Bele buche, neis bien asis,
Les surcilz bruns e bel le frunt
E le chef cresp e aukes blunt.   568
Fil d'or ne gette tel luur
Cum si cheval cuntre le jur.
Sis manteus fu de purpre bis,
Les pans en ot entur li mis.   572
Un espervier sur sun poin tient
E un levrer aprés lui vient.
Il n'ot al burc petit ne grant,
Ne li veillard ne li enfant,   576
Que ne l'alassent esgarder,

Si cum il la veent errer.
De sa beauté n'iert mie gas.
Ele veneit meins que le pas.   580
Li jugeür que la veeient
A grant merveille le teneient.
Il n'ot un sul ki l'esgardast
De dreite joie ne s'eschaufast.   584
Cil ki le chevaler amoent
A lui vienent, si li cuntouent
De la pucele ki veneit,
Si Deu plest, quel delivereit.   588
'Sire cumpain, ci en vient une,
Mes ele n'est pas fave ne brune;
Ceo est la plus bele del mund,
De tutes celes ke i sunt.'   592
Lanval l'oï, sun chief dresça,
Bien la cunut, si suspira;
Li sanc li est munté al vis.
De parler fu aukes hastifs: 596
'Par fei', fet il, 'ceo est m'amie.
Or m'en est gueres ki m'ocie,
Si ele n'ad merci de mei,
Kar gariz sui quant jeo la vei.'   600
La dame entra al palais;
Unc si bele n'i vient mais.
Devant le rei est descendue,
Si que de tuz iert bien veüe.   604
Sun mantel ad laissié chaeir,
Que meuz la puïssent veer.
Li reis, que mut fu enseigniez,
Il s'est encuntre li dresciez,   608
E tuit li autre l'enurerent;
De li servir se presenterent.
Quant il l'orent bien esgardee
E sa beauté forment loëe,   612
Ele parla en teu mesure,
Kar de demurer nen ot cure:
'Reis, j'ai amé un tuen vassal;
Veez le ici, ceo est Lanval.   616

Acheisuné fu en ta curt.
Ne vuil mie que a mal li turt
De ceo qu'il dist, ceo sachez tu,
Que la reïne ad tort eü.   620
Unques nul jur ne la requist.
De la vantance ke il fist,
Si par me peot estre aquitez,
Par voz baruns seit delivrez.'   624
Ceo qu'il en jugerunt par dreit
Li reis otrie ke issi seit;
N'i ad un sul que n'ait jugié
Que Lanval ad tut desrainié.   628
Delivrez est par lur esgart,
E la pucele s'en depart;
Ne la peot li reis retenir,
Asez gent ot a li servir.   632
Fors de la sale aveient mis
Un grant perrun de marbre bis,
U li pesant humme muntoent,
Que de la curt le rei aloent.   636
Lanval esteit munté desus.
Quant la pucele ist fors a l'us,
Sur le palefrei detriers li,
De plain eslais Lanval sailli.   640
Od li s'en vait en Avalun,
Ceo nus recontent li Bretun,
En un isle que mut est beaus;
La fu ravi li dameiseaus.   644
Nul hum n'en oï plus parler
Ne jeo n'en sai avant cunter.

LAÜSTIC

Une aventure vus dirai
Dunt li Bretun firent un lai.
Laüstic ad nun, ceo m'est vis,
Si l'apelent en lur païs;   4
Ceo est russignol en franceis
E nihtegale en dreit engleis.
En Seint Mallo en la cuntree
Ot une vile renumee.   8
Deus chevalers ilec manëent
E deus forz maisuns i aveient.
Pur la bunté des deus baruns
Fu de la vile bons li nuns.   12
Li uns aveit femme espusee,
Sage, curteise e acemee;
A merveille se teneit chiere
Sulunc l'usage e la manere.   16
Li autres fu un bachelers
Bien coneü entre ses pers
De pruësce, de grant valur,
E volenters feseit honur.   20
Mut turneot e despendeit
E bien donot ceo qu'il aveit.
La femme sun veisin ama.
Tant la requist, tant la preia   24
E tant par ot en lui grant bien
Que ele l'ama sur tute rien,
Tant pur le bien que ele oï,
Tant pur ceo qu'il iert pres de li.   28
Sagement e bien s'entr'amerent.
Mut se covrirent e garderent
Qu'il ne feussent aparceüz

Ne desturbez ne mescreüz;   32
E eus le poeient bien fere,
Kar pres esteient lur repere;
Preceines furent lur maisuns
E lur sales e lur dunguns.   36
N'i aveit bare ne devise
Fors un haut mur de piere bise.
Des chambres u la dame jut,
Quant a la fenestre s'estut,   40
Poeit parler a sun ami
De l'autre part e il a li,
E lur aveirs entrechangier
E par geter e par lancier.   44
N'unt gueres rien que lur despleise;
Mut esteient amdui a iese,
Fors tant k'il ne poënt venir
Del tut ensemble a lur pleisir;   48
Kar la dame ert estreit gardee,
Quant cil esteit en la cuntree.
Mes de tant aveient retur,
U fust par nuit u fust par jur,   52
Que ensemble poeient parler.
Nul nes poeit de ceo garder
Que a la fenestre n'i venissent
E iloec ne s'entreveïssent.   56
Lungement se sunt entr'amé,
Tant que ceo vient a un esté,
Que bruil e pré sunt reverdi
E li vergier ierent fluri.   60
Cil oiselet par grant duçur
Mainent lur joie en sum la flur.
Ki amur ad a sun talent
N'est merveille s'il i entent.   64
Del chevaler vus dirai veir:
Il i entent a sun poeir
E la dame de l'autre part,
E de parler e de regart.   68
Les nuiz, quant la lune luseit
E ses sires cuché esteit,

Dejuste lui sovent levot
E de sun mantel se afublot.   72
A la fenestre ester veneit,
Pur sun ami qu'el i saveit
Que autreteu vie demenot
E le plus de la nuit veillot.   76
Delit aveient al veer,
Quant plus ne poeient aver.
Tant i estut, tant i leva
Que ses sires s'en curuça   80
E meintefeiz li demanda
Pur quei levot e u ala.
'Sire', la dame li respunt,
'Il nen ad joie en cest mund   84
Ki n'ot le laüstic chanter.
Pur ceo me vois ici ester;
Tant ducement l'i oi la nuit
Que mut me semble grant deduit.   88
Tant me delit e tant le voil
Que jeo ne puis dormir de l'oil.'
Quant li sires ot que ele dist,
De ire e de maltalent en rist.   92
De une chose se purpensa:
Le laüstic enginnera.
Il n'ot vallet en sa meisun
Ne face engin, reis u laçun,   96
Puis les mettent par le vergier;
N'i ot codre ne chastainier
U il ne mettent laz u glu,
Tant que pris l'unt e retenu.   100
Quant le laüstic eurent pris,
Al seignur fu rendu tut vis.
Mut en fu liez quant il le tient;
As chambres a la dame vient.   104
'Dame', fet il, 'u estes vus?
Venez avant, parlez a nus!
J'ai le laüstic englué,
Pur quei vus avez tant veillé.   108
Desor poëz gisir en peis:

Il ne vus esveillerat meis.'
Quant la dame l'ad entendu,
Dolente e cureçuse fu. 112
A sun seignur l'ad demandé
E il l'ocist par engresté.
Le col li rumpt a ses deus meins;
De ceo fist il que trop vileins; 116
Sur la dame le cors geta,
Se que sun chainse ensanglanta
Un poi desur le piz devant.
De la chambre s'en ist atant. 120
La dame prent le cors petit;
Durement plure e si maudit
Ceus ki le laüstic traïrent
E les engins e laçuns firent, 124
Kar mut li unt toleit grant hait.
'Lasse', fet ele, 'mal m'estait!
Ne purrai mes la nuit lever
Ne aler a la fenestre ester, 128
U jeo suil mun ami veer.
Une chose sai jeo de veir:
Il quidera ke jeo me feigne;
De ceo m'estuet que cunseil preigne. 132
Le laüstic li trametrai,
L'aventure li manderai.'
En une piece de samit,
A or brusdé e tut escrit, 136
Ad l'oiselet envolupé.
Un sun vatlet ad apelé;
Sun message li ad chargié,
A sun ami l'ad enveié. 140
Cil est al chevalier venuz;
De part sa dame dist saluz,
Tut sun message li cunta,
Le laüstic li presenta. 144
Quant tut li ad dit e mustré
E il l'aveit bien escuté,
De l'aventure esteit dolenz,
Mes ne fu pas vileins ne lenz. 148

Un vasselet ad fet forgeer;
Unques n'i ot fer ne acer,
Tut fu de or fin od bones pieres,
Mut precïuses e mut cheres;   152
Covercle i ot tresbien asis.
Le laüstic ad dedenz mis,
Puis fist la chasse enseeler.
Tuz jurs l'ad fet od lui porter.   156
Cele aventure fu cuntee,
Ne pot estre lunges celee.
Un lai en firent li Bretun:
Le Laüstic l'apele hum.   160

CHEVREFOIL

Asez me plest e bien le voil,
Del lai qu'hum nume *Chevrefoil*,
Que la verité vus en cunt
Pur quei il fu fet e dunt.   4
Plusurs le m'unt cunté e dit
E jeo l'ai trové en escrit
De Tristram e de la reïne,
De lur amur que tant fu fine   8
Dunt il eurent meinte dolur,
Puis mururent en un jur.
Li reis Marks esteit curucié,
Vers Tristram sun nevuz irié.   12
De sa tere le cungea
Pur la reïne qu'il ama.
En sa cuntree en est alez,
En Suhtwales u il fu nez.   16
Un an demurat tut entier,
Ne pot ariere repeirier.
Mes puis se mist en abandun
De mort e de destructïun.   20
Ne vus esmerveilliez neent,
Kar ki eime lëalment
Mut est dolenz e trespensez
Quant il nen ad ses volentez.   24
Tristram est dolent e pensis;
Pur ceo se met de sun païs.
En Cornwaille vait tut dreit,
La u la reïne maneit.   28
En la forest tut sul se mist,
Ne voleit pas que hum le veïst.
En la vespree s'en eisseit,

Quant tens de herberger esteit. 32
Od païsanz, od povre gent,
Perneit la nuit herbergement.
Les noveles lur enquereit
Del rei cum il se cunteneit. 36
Ceo li dïent qu'il unt oï
Que li barun erent bani,
A Tintagel deivent venir.
Li reis i veolt sa curt tenir, 40
A Pentecuste i serunt tuit;
Mut i avra joie e deduit
E la reïne i sera.
Tristram l'oï, mut se haita: 44
Ele ne purrat mie aler
K'il ne la veie trespasser.
Le jur que li rei fu meüz,
E Tristram est al bois venuz, 48
Sur le chemin qu'il saveit
Que la rute passer deveit,
Une codre trencha par mi,
Tute quarreie la fendi. 52
Quant il ad paré le bastun,
De sun cutel escrit sun nun.
Se la reïne s'aparceit,
Que mut grant garde en perneit, 56
- Autre feiz li fu avenu
Que si l'aveit aparceü -
De sun ami bien conustra
Le bastun, quant el le verra. 60
Ceo fu la summe de l'escrit,
Qu'il li aveit mandé e dit
Que lunges ot ilec esté
E atendu e surjurné 64
Pur espïer e pur saver
Coment il la peüst veer,
Kar ne pot nent vivre sanz li.
D'euls deus fu il tut autresi 68
Cume del chevrefoil esteit
Ki a la codre se perneit.

Quant il s'i est laciez e pris
E tut entur le fust s'est mis, 72
Ensemble poënt bien durer.
Mes ki puis les volt desevrer,
Li codres muert hastivement
E li chevrefoil ensement. 76
'Bele amie, si est de nus:
Ne vus sanz mei ne mei sanz vus.'
La reïne vait chevachant;
Ele esgardat tut un pendant, 80
Le bastun vit, bien l'aparceut,
Tutes les lettres i conut.
Les chevalers que la menoënt,
Que ensemble od li erroënt, 84
Cumanda tuz a arester;
Descendre vot e resposer.
Cil unt fait sun cummandement.
Ele s'en vet luinz de sa gent; 88
Sa meschine apelat a sei,
Brenguein, que mut ot bone fei.
Del chemin un poi s'esluina;
Dedenz le bois celui trova 92
Que plus l'amot que rien vivant.
Entre eus meinent joie mut grant.
A li parlat tut a leisir
E ele li dit sun pleisir. 96
Puis li mustra cumfaitement
Del rei avrat acordement
E que mut li aveit pesé
De ceo qu'il l'ot si cungié; 100
Par encusement l'aveit fait.
A tant s'en part, sun ami lait;
Mes quant ceo vient al desevrer,
Dunc comencerent a plurer. 104
Tristram a Wales s'en rala
Tant que sis uncles le manda.
Pur la joie qu'il ot eüe
De s'amie qu'il ot veüe 108
E pur ceo k'il aveit escrit,

Si cum la reïne l'ot dit,
Pur les paroles remembrer,
Tristram, ki bien saveit harper,   112
En aveit fet un nuvel lai.
Asez briefment le numerai:
Gotelef l'apelent en engleis,
Chevrefoil le nument Franceis.   116
Dit vus en ai la verité
Del lai que j'ai ici cunté.

PENGUIN CLASSICS

www.penguinclassics.com

- Details about every Penguin Classic

- Advanced information about forthcoming titles

- Hundreds of author biographies

- FREE resources including critical essays on the books and their historical background, reader's and teacher's guides.

- Links to other web resources for the Classics

- Discussion area

- Online review copy ordering for academics

- Competitions with prizes, and challenging Classics trivia quizzes

PENGUIN CLASSICS ONLINE

READ MORE IN PENGUIN

In every corner of the world, on every subject under the sun, Penguin represents quality and variety – the very best in publishing today.

For complete information about books available from Penguin – including Puffins, Penguin Classics and Arkana – and how to order them, write to us at the appropriate address below. Please note that for copyright reasons the selection of books varies from country to country.

In the United Kingdom: Please write to *Dept. EP, Penguin Books Ltd, Bath Road, Harmondsworth, West Drayton, Middlesex UB7 0DA*

In the United States: Please write to *Consumer Services, Penguin Putnam Inc., 405 Murray Hill Parkway, East Rutherford, New Jersey 07073-2136.* VISA and MasterCard holders call 1-800-631-8571 to order Penguin titles

In Canada: Please write to *Penguin Books Canada Ltd, 10 Alcorn Avenue, Suite 300, Toronto, Ontario M4V 3B2*

In Australia: Please write to *Penguin Books Australia Ltd, 487 Maroondah Highway, Ringwood, Victoria 3134*

In New Zealand: Please write to *Penguin Books (NZ) Ltd, Private Bag 102902, North Shore Mail Centre, Auckland 10*

In India: Please write to *Penguin Books India Pvt Ltd, 11 Community Centre, Panchsheel Park, New Delhi 110017*

In the Netherlands: Please write to *Penguin Books Netherlands bv, Postbus 3507, NL-1001 AH Amsterdam*

In Germany: Please write to *Penguin Books Deutschland GmbH, Metzlerstrasse 26, 60594 Frankfurt am Main*

In Spain: Please write to *Penguin Books S. A., Bravo Murillo 19, 1°B, 28015 Madrid*

In Italy: Please write to *Penguin Italia s.r.l., Via Vittorio Emanuele 45/a, 20094 Corsico, Milano*

In France: Please write to *Penguin France, 12, Rue Prosper Ferradou, 31700 Blagnac*

In Japan: Please write to *Penguin Books Japan Ltd, Iidabashi KM-Bldg, 2-23-9 Koraku, Bunkyo-Ku, Tokyo 112 0004*

In South Africa: Please write to *Penguin Books South Africa (Pty) Ltd, P.O. Box 751093, Gardenview, 2047 Johannesburg*